Everyday Golf Psychology

Everyday Golf Psychology

Practical Advice for Golfers at Every Level

Jared Tendler, MS

JT PRESS

Softcover ISBN-13: 979-8-9941106-0-7
Hardcover ISBN-13: 978-1-7340309-9-0
Kindle ISBN-13: 979-8-9941106-8-3
Ebook ISBN-13: 979-8-9941106-9-0

Published by JT Press
www.jaredtendler.com

Cover design by Victoria Haidar
Book design by Karen Minster
Author photo by Kevin Peragine

PRINTED IN THE UNITED STATES

Contents

Contents

CRACKS IN THE FOUNDATION

CHAPTER 1

Holding the Club Upside Down

"Reverse every natural instinct and do the opposite
of what you are inclined to do, and you will probably
come very close to having a perfect golf swing."

— BEN HOGAN

I want you to picture something both simple and ridiculous. Imagine your playing partner stepping onto the first tee, putting down their bag, and settling in over the ball with the club held upside down.

You'd probably laugh, stare, or check for hidden cameras. But once you saw that your companion was serious, you'd shout for them to stop or step in and tackle them. Anything to prevent them from striking a shot with the club inverted.

Now here's the uncomfortable part: That's how you, and most golfers, approach the mental game.

Not literally, of course. But metaphorically, you're doing the same thing. Your perspective on what matters, what improves performance, what creates consistency, what derails you under pressure... it's all backward. *You're holding the club upside down.* And because the mental game is invisible, no one taps you on the shoulder to correct your grip.

In the quote that opens this chapter, Ben Hogan was talking about mechanics, but he could just as easily have been writing a thesis on golf psychology. Little in this game rewards the instinctive reaction. What feels natural—trying harder, thinking more, tightening up, forcing confidence, getting angry, "fixing" your swing mid-round, protecting a good score—is almost always the thing that makes your golf worse.

And just as you can't build a reliable swing with a bad grip or poor alignment, you can't build reliable performance on a warped perspective. You might pull off good shots, even good rounds, while compensating for improper fundamentals, but it always catches up to you. The same is true mentally. If your understanding of confidence, pressure, luck, focus, or emotion is flawed, you're going to be compensating on every shot. You might survive for a while, but you can't thrive. Not with the club held upside down in your mind.

You've probably heard the saying "golf is 90 percent mental." It's an industry refrain, repeated everywhere from driving ranges to instruction books and beyond. Want to know something? It's dead wrong.

A 20-handicap won't become scratch simply by improving their mentality. There are instances when your golf game feels mostly mental, but the game isn't that way. We don't hit the ball with our mind. Golf is a physical sport. Physical capability is foremost.

Golf isn't 90 percent mental. Not even close. At least not the golf that most of us play. If it were, golf psychologists would be positioned at every course alongside swing instructors.

I suspect our backward thinking about the mental game stems partly from a famous quote from the legendary Bobby Jones: "Golf is played mainly on a five-and-a-half-inch course … the space between your ears." Except that's not exactly what he said. Jones was referring to "competitive" golf. Almost invariably, the word "competitive" is omitted from the quote. At the highest levels of the game, where little separates players' physical gifts, golf may in fact be 90 percent mental. No doubt, Jones's control of his mind and emotions gave him a crucial edge over his opponents. The same could be said of Tiger Woods at his peak. And Scottie Scheffler today.

But that's not how golf works for the rest of us. The misleading quote has fed a false narrative, convincing generations of golfers that the key to improvement is simply thinking the right way. As if the ideal mindset were a light switch you could flip on before a round. As if wanting it more, expecting your best, or saying the right words to yourself could magically change the result. For those of us not named Jones or Woods or Scheffler, the mental game matters. Of course it does. But we've got the wrong ideas about how to wield it.

Those misunderstandings have created a whole ecosystem of bad assumptions and counterproductive habits:

- Overreacting to bad shots or breaks

- Flag hunting when you know not to

- Being psyched out by hazards and out-of-bounds

- Focusing too much on score and swing

- Rushing and compounding mental mistakes

- Lacking concentration

- Forcing, pressing, expecting too much

Truth is, most players spend their entire golfing lives fighting battles that don't need to be fought in the first place. They assume their inconsistency is only mechanical. They assume their bad rounds happen because something is wrong with their equipment. They assume that pressure and nerves and frustration are signs of weakness rather than features of the game that can be understood, managed, and corrected. They assume they're lost because they're not strong enough—when, in reality, they're lost because no one ever taught them how the mind works.

This book exists to correct that.

Not by offering platitudes or motivational slogans or cute acronyms. Not by telling you to "be positive" or "stay calm" or "believe in yourself." You've heard all that. It only scratches the surface.

Instead, we're going to do something much more practical and much more powerful: We're going to rebuild your mental approach from the ground up. But unlike overhauling your swing, it won't take years.

In the chapters ahead, you'll learn how to actually thrive under pressure, how confidence is built (and destroyed), why focus is misunderstood, why emotional control fails when you need it most, why decision-making breaks down on the course, and how to focus less on score and swing.

Nothing in this book requires special talent. Nothing requires superhuman discipline. And nothing requires that you become a different person. You don't need to be calmer, tougher, smarter, or more spiritual. You just need a mental approach that isn't upside down.

By the time you're done with these pages, you'll know how to:

- Handle pressure instead of fearing it

- Prevent frustration from blowing up your round

- Avoid getting ahead of yourself or thinking too much about score

- Build confidence that lasts longer than one good shot

- Make committed decisions that hold up under stress

- Recover from mistakes without spiraling

- Take your game from the range to the course

- Play to your actual potential, not your theoretical one

You'll understand why you sabotage yourself, why your performance swings so wildly, and why your best golf shows up at random instead of on command. And you'll learn how to produce the version of your golf that feels natural, repeatable, and honest—the version that reflects what you're truly capable of, not what your instincts trick you into doing.

Before we go any further, let's return to that image from the first tee—your friend gripping the club by the face. It's an absurd picture, but it's also the perfect metaphor for how most golfers navigate the mental side of the game. They're trying hard. They're well-intentioned. They want to play well. But they're starting from the wrong end entirely.

This book is about flipping the club. It's about turning your perspective right-side up so you can finally play the game as it's meant to be played—not perfectly, but with your full ability available to you.

Everything that follows is designed to help you do exactly that.

Let's begin.

CHAPTER 2

A Model of Consistency

"You have to spend time on your weaknesses.
When I was young I used to spend time on the things
I was good at. I would forget all the other things."
— ANNIKA SÖRENSTAM

The inconsistency of your game is torturous. How is it possible to play so differently from one round to the next, or even one hole to the next? How can you block a tee shot so far O.B. it needs a passport, then stripe the reload like a pro? How do you post one of your best rounds of the year and follow it a few days later with a personal lowlight?

The ups and downs make you crave consistency. You don't expect to shoot your handicap every time. You understand the game is fickle: bad bounces, burned edges, unfriendly lies. What bothers you isn't golf's unpredictability. It's your volatility.

You know what you're capable of when you play well. You don't need to reinvent your swing; you just want your good shots to show up more often and your disasters to happen less. Those are reasonable goals. So you take lessons, pound range balls, buy new clubs, switch balls, cycle through putters, binge tips on YouTube, read books. Anything and everything in search of consistency, which still eludes you.

You're not necessarily searching in the wrong places. You're just searching with the wrong perspective. To become truly consistent, you need to rethink what consistency actually is.

Consistent Within a Range

As a thought experiment, imagine rating every shot you've hit in the past 6 to 18 months on a scale from 1 (worst) to 10 (best). Plot those numbers and you'd see a bell curve. Don't worry. This isn't a statistics lesson. The picture matters more than the math.

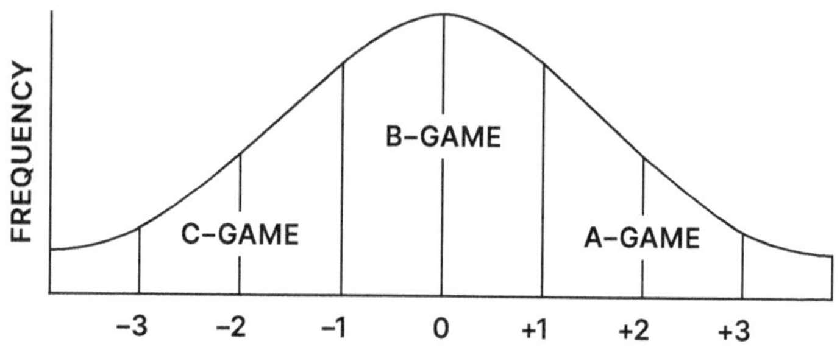

On the right side of the curve live your best shots—your A-game. On the left, your worst—your C-game. In the middle sits the version of you that shows up most often—your B-game. Everyone has their own curve, sometimes shifted to the right during hot stretches, sometimes sagging left during slumps.

I'm not asking you to actually graph this. That's not necessary. You already have a feel for yours.

The important question: Which part of the curve do you think represents your game?

Odds are, your view does not reflect reality. Some golfers mentally erase their worst shots, pretending their A-game is the "real" them. Others, when struggling, see nothing but the left side of the curve and forget their A-game still exists at all. Both distortions make your game look far more mystifying than it actually is.

Your real game isn't just one part, it's the whole picture.

The true measure of consistency isn't how good your best shots are. It's the size of the gap between your best and worst: the distance from A-game to C-game. The steadiest players have narrow gaps. These are the golfers you hate facing in a match. Their worst is still workable. They don't blow up. They don't beat themselves. You have to earn a win against them.

It's often said that golf is a game of misses, and that minimizing them is central to success. That's true. When inconsistency plagues you, your C-game misses are simply too big, too damaging. And while it's tempting to obsess over your A-game—it's fun to remember the 4-iron you flushed to three feet on 18—it's a trap. In his prime, Tiger Woods famously talked about scoring well without his A-game. He often sounded as pleased by those rounds as he was when he'd been firing on all cylinders. That's because he understood that in golf, managing the gap is how to maximize your peak.

Trying to boost your A-game can be counterproductive. It can actually widen that gap. Your bad shots feel worse. Your emotions swing harder. Your scoring grows more streaky. You fatigue faster. Consistency doesn't come from polishing your best. It comes from upgrading your worst.

C-Game Builds Consistency

Contrary to popular belief, your C-game—not your A-game— is where true command is forged. When you know your "bad" can only get so bad, you swing with more confidence on tight tee shots, stay calmer when a low number is on the horizon, and feel less self-conscious playing with better golfers.

Your C-game is the backbone of your game. The old line about a team being only as strong as its weakest link applies here too. Your improvement hinges on your willingness to actually look at, understand, and tackle that weak link. Ignoring it doesn't make it go away. In fact, many golfers have unintentionally held themselves back for years by refusing to acknowledge their C-game honestly.

All golfers, even Tour pros, have a C-game. Perfection appears in small bursts, but no one is immune to poor shots. What varies is how bad those poor shots are.

And yet, many golfers respond to their misses in predictable, unhelpful ways:

- They avoid practicing weaker skills because it's more fun to chase distance

- They assume they already know how to eliminate chunks, skulls, slices, or shanks

- They rationalize their worst shots as flukes— "That's not like me"—and move on without understanding them

- They try to improve their C-game, but do so haphazardly

The goal isn't to accept your weaknesses and feel at peace with them. The goal is to strengthen them. Consistency comes from making your C-game less destructive. Put bluntly, you need to find ways to suck less.

When you're struggling, the instinct is to force greatness, but forcing greatness rarely produces greatness. It usually deepens the struggle. Focusing on "sucking less," however, lowers expectations and makes the next shot feel manageable again. It shifts your mindset from "I need a miracle" to "Let's just be a little better than that last one."

Apply that mentality round after round and the small wins stack up. You gradually eliminate the mistakes that used to wreck your scorecard. You handle pressure better. You avoid the big numbers that once defined your off days. Your C-game edges upward, narrowing the gap to your A-game.

In your next few rounds, watch for the moments where things start to slide, those unsettling situations that typically trigger your C-game. Then find one small way to be a little better: loosen your grip, take an extra beat to read the speed of a putt, pick a more precise target.

Some of you will see improvement immediately. Others will simply become more aware of your C-game. That awareness is improvement, even if it doesn't feel like it. You can't fix what you can't see.

While something in your technique may contribute to bad shots, the underlying cause is often mental or emotional. Mechanics don't exist in a vacuum. They're influenced by tension, frustration, nerves, overconfidence, slow play, low energy, or fear of certain holes. Many golfers don't need a swing overhaul to reduce their C-game; they need a mindset adjustment.

The rest of this book will help you identify those mental tendencies and shift them, so you can move your C-game forward and become the more consistent player you've always wanted to be.

KEY TAKEAWAYS

Being consistent doesn't mean always playing your best, it means having a narrow gap between your A-game and C-game.

To become more consistent, you must find a way to hit slightly better shots at times you typically struggle. That's how you narrow the gap between the best and worst parts of your game.

CHAPTER 3

Finding "It" Without Falling for "It"

"The minute you think you've got the
game licked, it jumps up and bites you."

— SAM SNEAD

There's nothing like hitting a perfect golf shot. You flush a drive and watch it soar through the blue sky, or pure an iron so cleanly you barely feel the strike. Moments like these deepen our love for the game and keep us coming back for more.

They're especially sweet when you've been struggling—grinding on the range, fighting your swing—and then suddenly something clicks. Perfection. All the frustration melts away as you revel in the glory of your success, wondering why it took 16 holes to find it.

In the last chapter, I wrote about moving your C-game forward. This is the flip side: reaching a new A-game. Maybe you've just had a breakthrough after a lesson, a tip from a friend, or a flash of insight like Hogan digging answers out of the dirt. When that happens, it feels almost magical. You've solved the puzzle. Or so you think.

For a while, it might even last: flush contact, laser focus, putts dropping center cup. This new version of your game feels like your new normal. You know golf is fickle, and yet there's a small voice that whispers: *Maybe this time, it's permanent.*

Wouldn't it be amazing if you could stay there forever?

Or would it?

In a classic *Twilight Zone* episode called "A Nice Place to Visit," a bank robber dies in a shootout with the cops and awakens in a world where he gets everything he ever wanted—a mansion, beautiful women, every pull of the slot machine a win. At first, he believes he's in heaven. But after a month, he's bored and miserable. The thrill is gone; the challenge has vanished. The twist: He's actually in hell, condemned to get everything he wants forever.

Golf offers the same paradox. The idea of permanently finding "it" is seductive, but if you truly did, the game would lose its meaning. There would be nothing left to chase, no mystery, no growth. The struggle gives us joy. (Also makes great fodder for post-round griping.)

That longing for "it" isn't irrational. It's human. It comes from the part of us that wants to create magic in the world. Over time, that same motivation drives real progress. Imagine Old Tom Morris seeing today's game—the equipment, the course conditions, the precision. He'd be astonished. Magic happens collectively, over generations, not one range session.

You can create your own version of that magic too, not by chasing a single breakthrough, but by realizing there are always more "its" ahead—more small breakthroughs to discover. Each time you push your limits, you move your A-game forward. The trick is doing it without losing balance. And what's the key to that? The answer lies in an unlikely source: the inchworm. Yeah, that's right. Keep reading.

The Inchworm Concept

If you've ever watched an inchworm move, you know the pattern: it stretches forward, anchors the front, then pulls the back end up—inch by inch. Inchworms aren't fast. You wouldn't want to be caught behind a foursome of them. But that's not the point. The point is their shape. Picture a bell curve moving the same way.

Your game has a similar curve: your A-game at the front, your C-game at the back. Improvement happens inchworm-style— first a push forward (your A-game improving), then a pull from the back (your C-game getting less bad). Over time, the whole curve moves forward.

But if you only chase the front end—always searching for "it"—your C-game stays put. The gap widens, and soon you feel like two different golfers: the one who shoots 74 one day and 88 the next. That's the cost of falling for "it."

How do you know if your game has been stretched thin? Here are telltale signs that the gap between your A- and C-games has grown too wide:

- You dismiss bad rounds with "that's not like me" instead of learning from them

- You feel like your own worst enemy in certain stretches

- You practice a lot but still have blowup days that make no sense

- You cling to routines because your game feels fragile without them

- You can't stay in the zone for long—or reach it at all

When your A- and C-games drift too far apart, the only fix is from the back. Focus first on narrowing that gap. Once your foundation is stronger, your A-game can advance sustainably.

When you're playing great, remember that your C-game is still lurking. Since you'll always have a C-game, keep upgrading it. Don't fear it—just remain aware of it. Confidence turns to overconfidence the moment you forget it's there, opening the door for your C-game to return.

Working with Your A-, B-, and C-Games

Most golfers are naturally drawn to their A-game—it's fun to chase, and progress feels obvious. But when you discover something new, resist the urge to force it. Early breakthroughs are fragile. Forcing them is like making a toddler run before they can walk. Let them settle in. Don't try to control the motion—trust it, observe it, and let your natural athleticism do the work by focusing on the shot, not the move. True control comes later, from your B-game.

Improving your B-game, by contrast, is often tedious. It's where you find consistency, not magic. But it's the glue that holds your game together. Apply both mental and technical upgrades. If you practice a lot, improving your B-game is likely the bulk of what you already work on; just make sure the progress transfers to the course. If you don't practice much, that's okay—you can still strengthen your B-game by resisting the pull of your C-game when things go sideways. Every time you maintain focus, nail your setup, or recover composure instead of spiraling, you make your B-game stronger.

It doesn't take perfection; just persistence. Like training a muscle, each small act of resistance adds up. Especially when the difficulty grows. Push yourself to be a little better, or just less terrible, and you forge new strength, which eventually leads to your C-game inching forward.

A little preparation is all it takes to suck less and start transforming your game. To see if you're ready, try this test: Give yourself 30 seconds to describe how you'd correct your common C-game mistakes on the course. Ready, go.

How'd you do? Probably not great. I often spring this on my clients to test their readiness. If you hesitate or draw a blank, you're not prepared. C-game moments strike when your mind is already spinning—when you're tired, frustrated, distracted, feeling pressure, or pressing too hard. That's no time to invent the right thought or swing cue. You can't expect to make mechanical or mental adjustments spontaneously on the course.

The key is readiness. Instead, plan for it. Write down a few simple reminders on an index card, your scorecard, or a phone note.

"Pick a clear target."

"Stay in posture."

"Tempo first."

Small cues like these can rescue you when things start to wobble. You can't simulate those high-pressure moments in practice—the course is where that learning happens. Each time you handle one of those moments just a little better, you build the reps needed to eventually move your back end forward permanently. A few seconds of preparation can save you countless strokes, and a lot of frustration, in those tough moments. That's how your bell curve advances.

The beauty of golf is that "it" always comes and goes. Every flash of perfection is fleeting, but also an invitation to grow. The goal isn't to find "it" and hold on—it's to keep moving, inch by inch, toward a better version of yourself. The search never ends. That's not a curse. That's the magic. And there's always more of it to come.

KEY TAKEAWAYS

Golf would be boring if you truly found "it" permanently.

You can find more "its" by improving both the front and the back of your bell curve—moving forward like an inchworm.

Prepare to battle your C-game with a simple reminder to help you handle tough moments on the course.

CHAPTER 4

Changing Your Mindset is Easy

"No matter how good you are, you can always get better,
and that's the exciting part."
— TIGER WOODS

Deep down, you know you can play better. At some level, every golfer does.

You also know that improvement in golf rarely happens like magic. There's a process. You understand that too. Tweaking your swing, refining your short game, or dialing in your putting takes practice. You put in the reps, see what works on the course, get feedback, and practice some more. Improvement takes practice.

Yet when it comes to your thoughts, emotions, decision-making, focus, and other aspects of golf psychology, progress is treated differently. You rarely hear about the actual process of improving on this side of the game, which is odd, because the stages you instinctively recognize on the physical side apply here too.

Clearly, you can't transform your swing overnight, just as you can't bulk up just by reading a fitness book. But there's an even more persistent illusion in golf: that you can become calm, patient, and confident just from a tip from a friend or by reading a book…wink, wink. Sure, it could happen. You could also win the lottery. But you probably shouldn't bank on it.

And that's where the term "mindset" can mislead you. It implies you can get your mind set right quickly and permanently.

I prefer the term mental game, because you engage in a learning process, just like any other game. That learning process never ends. You can call it what you want; the key is how you approach it. The best advice in the world is useless if you don't view learning correctly.

To make it easier, I'll explain a simple framework and give you practical guidance that will help you learn more effectively.

The Four Stages of Learning

Learning unfolds in stages, each with a distinct start and finish. Think of learning to drive a car. At first, you're acutely aware of every action—steering, signaling, checking mirrors. Over time, you face more scenarios, your reactions become smoother, and eventually many decisions become automatic. The mechanics become second nature.

Golf works the same way. When you're learning a swing, you focus on grip, stance, takeaway. Later, those basics support more advanced goals: hitting different distances, adjusting to conditions, improving accuracy. While players differ in pace and where they get stuck, learning follows a predictable path. The "Adult Learning Model"[1] defines four stages of learning:

STAGE 1: Unconscious Incompetence
You don't know what you don't know. This isn't necessarily bad—sometimes ignorance is bliss. But if you're unaware that anger, distraction, or overconfidence is creeping into your game, that's a problem you need to recognize.

STAGE 2: Conscious Incompetence

You're aware of what you don't know or where you struggle. Awareness gives you the chance to improve, but it doesn't make you skilled. You've identified the problem; now comes the work.

STAGE 3: Conscious Competence

You've developed skill through practice and can apply it on the course. But there's a catch: you need enough energy and emotional stability to execute consistently. Under stress or fatigue, you can slip back to the previous stage.

STAGE 4: Unconscious Competence

You've mastered the skill so thoroughly that it's automatic, even under pressure, distraction, or fatigue. But be aware: this also includes old habits you're good at but don't want to be. Learning is neutral. It knows what's trained, not whether that training improves your game.

Progress through these stages isn't linear. You'll often take steps forward and backward as you bring what you've practiced to the course—steadily inching toward Unconscious Competence.

Knowing where aspects of your mental game reside in the stages of learning helps inform what you do next. Too many of you don't realize that you're only at the level of Conscious Incompetence with many aspects of your mental game. While you know the right way to handle bad breaks, slow play, or poor shots, overreacting to a perfect drive in a divot, a playing partner who is never ready to hit, or chunking an approach shot in the water proves that you haven't reached Unconscious Competence. Aim for mastery, not just basic competence.

Training corrections to Unconscious Competence is how your C-game permanently moves forward. This frees your mind from the burden of thinking. You no longer need conscious effort. The upgrade has been automated. It's easier to perform well and you have space to learn something new.

Understanding these stages helps you learn more efficiently and avoid setbacks. Think of it like a sandcastle, washed away by waves. It's frustrating to see your hard work undone, but you can rebuild stronger. That's how lasting improvement works. You can achieve that by avoiding these common learning pitfalls:

Doing Too Much at Once

Many golfers try to fix everything at once: pre-shot routine, swing mechanics, decision-making, wedge control, and emotional resilience. The mind can only handle so much at a time. (More on this in Chapter 9.) Mastery is competence without thinking. Conscious effort burns much more energy. Overloading leads to fatigue, frustration, and setbacks. Knock down one challenge at a time, or tackle the biggest problem first and get it out of the way. Either approach works.

When Focus is a Placebo

Let's say your biggest problem is the first tee. You struggle with the pressure, often hitting terrible tee shots even after you've been striping it on the range. Then you get a tip or try a new technique and next time out, you see immediate improvement. Not only did you hit a better opening shot, you also felt more relaxed. Success! If this change continues to work, great. But if it fades, it might have been a placebo—the improvement came from novelty or expectation rather than a real correction. Don't despair. Don't assume failure if progress disappears. Get reps in. Test, experiment, and find the corrections that actually stick.

Tripping at the Finish Line

The intangible nature of the mental game makes the finish line hard to spot. The race isn't over until progress appears easily under tough circumstances. The correction must become your default reaction. Don't get ahead of yourself. Even when you know the right response, you can still take steps backward—missing a short putt under pressure, compounding a poor shot with a bad decision. This isn't failure; this is the final stretch before Unconscious Competence. Keep your corrections fresh. Each small improvement—handling pressure slightly better, getting a bit less frustrated—compounds over time.

If this chapter feels abstract, revisit it after identifying the specific mental-game corrections you want to focus on. The stages of learning will make more sense once you start addressing a specific problem.

———

KEY TAKEAWAYS

Improving your mental game happens, like the golf swing, in stages, not overnight.

Just "knowing" the right way to react isn't enough. Train the upgrades to your mentality, expecting ups and downs as you progress toward Unconscious Competence.

Unconscious Competence removes the burden of conscious effort, freeing your mind to be more athletic or improve another area of your game.

CHAPTER 5

Eliminate Negative Thinking

"Sometimes we get so afraid of hitting bad shots
we don't let ourselves hit good ones."
— BUTCH HARMON

Negative thoughts can be tormenting, distracting, and often relentless. Whether they appear spontaneously or well before you arrive at the course, you know what it's like when your own thoughts seem to turn against you. A harassing voice pipes up:

"Don't go in the water."

"Don't chunk it in the bunker."

"Don't embarrass yourself out there."

Almost instantly, tension rises, and you try to fight those thoughts. But you still can't help imagining how stupid you'll feel hitting it in the water, the bunker, or pull-hooking the first tee shot.

You argue with yourself, get mad for even thinking like this, and then get even more frustrated when you hit the very shot you were trying to avoid. Or, just as often, you get so tense fixating on one bad outcome that you manufacture a bad shot of an entirely different flavor.

Negative thoughts can also strike suddenly in the middle of your swing. You think "don't go right" at the top of your backswing and instinctively pull it left. Or as you take the putter back on a three-footer, "don't miss it" pops into your head. Despite feeling confident just moments earlier, you jab at the ball and miss.

These thoughts often arrive in rapid-fire succession. It's remarkable how many you can have in such a short period of time, and how negative they can be for seemingly no reason. You're out there doing your best, and this disruptive inner voice is trying to psych you out. It can feel like you're quietly sabotaging your own efforts to play good golf.

Eager to put an end to this chaos, you may have followed the prevailing wisdom: Negative thoughts can't be eliminated, so don't engage them—let them pass like a leaf blowing in the wind. Sometimes this works. Other times it doesn't. And when it fails, it can make things worse, leaving you even more frustrated that you can't stop yourself from being negative.

Prevailing wisdom, however, is not your only option. When you understand the different reasons your mind produces negative thoughts, you can gain far more control over them, even stopping them before they start. They only seem uncontrollable now because trying to stop them directly is like trying to square the clubface at impact by flipping your hands. You can do it, but it's harder, less reliable, and much more likely to fail under pressure.

To develop reliable face control, instructors focus on setup, takeaway, downswing. In other words, what happens before impact largely determines what happens at impact. In the same way, the key to controlling negative thoughts is often determined by what you do before they ever show up.

To begin, let's look at why negative thoughts occur in the first place. Many golfers treat them as one big problem, but understanding the differences is essential to gaining real control.

Negative Thoughts Are a Distraction

Have you hit quality shots or made putts with negative thoughts in your head? Yes. While you may not easily recall those instances, there have been times when you've done it. We tend to remember the moments when negative thoughts got the best of us, and forget the times they didn't.

Negative thoughts don't cause you to hit bad shots. The problem begins when they consume your focus or force you to focus on where you don't want the ball to go. Both are distractions. The more you feed them, the more they pull your attention away from the shot at hand.

Sometimes players joke that the mind doesn't know the word "no" because when you tell yourself "don't go in the bunker," "don't slice it in the trees," or "don't skull it over the green," the ball seems to end up in the exact place you're trying to avoid. Obviously, you understand what "no" means. That's not the issue. You're simply more likely to hit the ball where your focus is directed.

The body has an incredible ability to produce outcomes that follow your focus. You've spent years training your body for golf, developing the power, agility, and precision needed to hit a wide variety of shots. This athleticism—often called muscle memory—responds to what you're focused on. When pitching to a short-sided pin over a bunker, the more you focus on dumping it in the sand, the more your body is primed to decelerate at impact and send the ball exactly where your attention is aimed.

Negative thoughts are far less consequential than bad focus. You're at your best when you're focused on the shot or putt you're trying to hit. Think of yourself as distracted when you're overly focused on where you don't want the ball to go, or when you're so absorbed in the negative chatter in your head that you can't focus on your target. That kind of distraction is no different than hitting a shot while thinking about your feet or some other irrelevant detail.

Treat negative thoughts like a distraction. Train your mind to focus more on the shot you want to hit and less on the outcome you want to avoid. This approach allows you to stop fighting negative thoughts directly, which only diverts more attention away from the task at hand.

If this feels difficult at first, remember the advice from the previous chapter. You're in the Conscious Incompetence stage, and with repetition it will become easier to regain command of your focus. However, if you don't see progress after a few weeks, that's a sign your negative thinking may be driven by one of the other causes we're about to explore.

Negativity Can Highlight Weakness

Negative thoughts can also serve a useful purpose: highlighting weaknesses in your game. You might worry about blading a chip shot when chipping is the weakest part of your game, or struggle with negative thoughts in windy conditions if you have trouble controlling trajectory.

When you have command of your game, negativity is less likely. When you lack command of a shot or situation, it's reasonable to feel uneasy. The question isn't whether the shot is hard. It's how you respond to that fact.

Many golfers don't like to admit weakness. You can joke about it or be outwardly self-deprecating, but negativity often shows up when you haven't fully accepted the weaker parts of your game.

Denial doesn't silence negativity. It strengthens it. Your subconscious knows the truth. If a 70-yard wedge shot over water is difficult because you tend to take the club back too far and decelerate at impact, it's no surprise that "don't chunk it" dominates your thoughts. Denying that weakness costs energy and focus, both of which would be better spent executing the shot.

Here's a simpler approach: When negative thoughts arise, acknowledge that the shot is hard for you right now. No judgment. Then either choose a safer option or take the challenge head on. When you make it clear that you're rising to the challenge, you encourage yourself to be bold, a mentality that makes it easier to move past negative thoughts.

Regardless of the result, the acknowledged difficulty of the shot creates room for productive feedback. You can recognize solid execution even if the outcome wasn't perfect, and you reinforce the fact that you didn't shy away.

Recognizing that a shot is hard is just information. You might struggle with sidehill lies, fairway bunker shots, or short left-to-right putts. That's normal. Every golfer has weaknesses. But when negative thoughts arise and you deny them, you're expecting more from your game than it can reliably deliver.

In golf, admitting weakness is an advantage. There are countless ways to get the ball in the hole. Sometimes that means laying back off the tee or aiming for the center of the green with a three-quarter shot rather than forcing a low-percentage play.

Golf's difficulty is a large part of its appeal. Far more people play chess than checkers because they're drawn to the endless complexity. Golf has a similar allure. (That's why we like it more than mini golf.) Its complexity engages the mind, drives us to be better, and rewards us when we conquer another challenge. Each weakness you acknowledge is an opportunity to improve.

If you apply these ideas and negativity still blares loudly in your mind, it's likely those thoughts aren't simply distractions or useful signals. They're probably reflexes driven by emotion.

Negative Thinking as a Reflex

When a doctor taps your knee with a rubber hammer, your leg jumps without conscious control. In the same way, your mind can respond to certain golf situations with instant negative thoughts—not because you're thinking, but because you're reacting.

These reactions are fast, automatic, and familiar. There's no novelty to them. They arise as part of a broader emotional response in your mind and body. For example:

> After a few poor tee shots, you berate yourself: "How can I practice so much and still be this bad?" and you're certain the next one will be awful.

> You see O.B. down the right side, your body tightens, your focus scatters, and "don't slice it" jumps into your mind—followed shortly by a slice.

> You lose the first two holes of a match against a tough opponent and, walking to the third tee, think, "I might not win a hole."

You're playing well but grow increasingly frustrated by bad breaks and can't stop thinking, "My score should be so much lower."

These aren't "thoughts" in the traditional sense. Thinking is slow and deliberate, like deciding which club to hit from an awkward lie. What we're calling negative thoughts here are automatic responses tied to emotion.

That's why they're so difficult to control. The more you try to suppress them, the more emotional pressure builds, until it overwhelms your ability to stay composed. Trying to control emotionally driven negative thoughts is a losing battle, especially under pressure or when you're tired.

This is why conventional strategies can work temporarily. Deep breaths, distraction, or focusing on your surroundings can reduce emotional intensity in the moment. You can continue to use these tactics, but it helps to recognize that negative thoughts are signals of emotion, not enemies you need to defeat.

The limitation of simply letting thoughts pass is that it's a Band-Aid. You'll need it again and again, and it's most likely to fail when the emotion behind the thoughts becomes strongest.

Lasting change comes from addressing the source. When you uncover and correct the emotional causes behind these reflexive responses, the trigger for negative thinking loses its power. Remove the emotion, and the thoughts fade with it.

That's how negative thinking is truly reduced—and often eliminated. In the next chapter, we'll look closely at how emotions hijack your game, and what you can do to regain control.

KEY TAKEAWAYS

Negative thoughts don't cause bad shots. Your swing follows your focus. Steadily train your mind to focus more on where you want the ball to go.

Negativity isn't bad when it helps you recognize when a challenging shot needs either a safer choice or a bold mentality.

Instant and repetitive negative thoughts are tied to emotions. Correct the source of the emotion and negative thinking loses its power.

CHAPTER 6

Technique to Control Emotion

"A bad attitude is worse than a bad swing."
— PAYNE STEWART

Emotions are inherent to golf. The game has highs and lows, excitement and despair, often in the same round. Bad breaks and missed opportunities cause frustration and anger. Anxiety surges on the first tee. Nerves strike on the last green over a meaningful putt. You're elated when you pull off an amazing recovery shot, shocked by a cruel lip-out, and impatient behind a slow group.

Like playing in a stiff breeze, it's hard to play well when your emotions are swirling. You're doing your best, but emotions can outplay you. That's often the result of unreliable and inconsistent attempts at controlling them—blocking them out, loosening up with a drink, taking deep breaths, or leaning heavily on a pre-shot routine. You try to manage emotion, but you don't train a technique you can rely on.

You may also assume emotions are the problem, when the opposite is true: they're actually a requirement. When you're playing great, you might feel calm and relaxed, but that's not the same state you're in watching TV on the couch. Emotion fuels performance. Motivation, interest, and passion create the intensity, focus, and presence of mind behind your best rounds.

Negative emotions can do this too. Anger and anxiety aren't inherently bad. Sometimes frustration sharpens your focus. Some players thrive under pressure and struggle without it.

Labeling these emotions as "bad" ignores clear evidence that they can elevate performance. Just be cautious. They're powerful tools, but volatile ones, especially in untrained hands.

Emotion isn't the problem; excess emotion is. At the right level, emotion is useful. When it rises too high, chaos follows—extra nerves lead to tight grips, irritation causes poor decisions, excitement after a birdie leads you to swing too hard on the next tee. There's a reason the term "post-birdie curse" exists. Excess emotion causes obvious mistakes—things you know better than to do but can't stop yourself from doing. That's what inconsistent emotional control costs you.

Some players have partial systems that work occasionally; others manage emotions without realizing it. Common examples include:

After a bad round or before a tournament, you tell yourself, "At the end of the day it's just golf. There's nothing to worry about—just go play." By pretending not to care as much, you're trying to blunt frustration or fear.

When your mind jumps ahead to posting a career low, you repeatedly tell yourself to "just focus on the present."

Facing a shot over water, you cling tightly to your pre-shot routine, executing it as precisely as possible to manage anxiety.

After carelessly giving away a few shots, you try to stay positive, reminding yourself that "everyone has bad holes—you can make it up on the next one."

When your game is off, you chalk it up to "not being your day," blaming conditions, wind, or slow play in hopes of resetting for the next round.

You demand perfect silence over the ball and/or take extra time to hit, waiting until you feel completely comfortable before pulling the trigger.

These tactics aren't wrong. They can help in the short term. But they're crutches. Break your ankle and crutches are useful. But the goal is to walk unassisted. With emotional control, crutches prevent you from building strength. They often fail when emotions are stronger, like in money games, tournaments, or when paired with better players. And they limit growth: How can you run if you still need help walking?

To build a reliable technique for controlling emotion, you need to understand one critical rule.

Malfunctioning Mind

The brain operates in a hierarchy that gives emotion more power than rational thought. When emotions become too intense, they can shut down thinking, awareness, decision-making, and your ability to regulate emotion itself. That's right. Intense emotions block emotional control.[2]

Emotional control is a mental process, which makes it vulnerable. This is simply how the brain is wired. We can't change it; we can only work within it.

When emotions spike, do you recognize any of the following?

- The game speeds up and you go on autopilot

- You fixate on trouble instead of targets

- You walk faster and rush your swing just to get the shot over with

- You lose your feel and stop trusting your reads

- You know what you're doing is wrong but can't stop

- Your mind goes blank at emotional extremes

These problems are inevitable unless you catch the rise of emotion early, before it intensifies. The stronger the emotion, the less control you have over it.

This relationship is described by the Yerkes-Dodson Law.[3] Performance peaks with the right level of emotion. Too little and you're flat. Too much and performance drops. The sweet spot lies in between. The following graph provides a good visual of this balancing act.

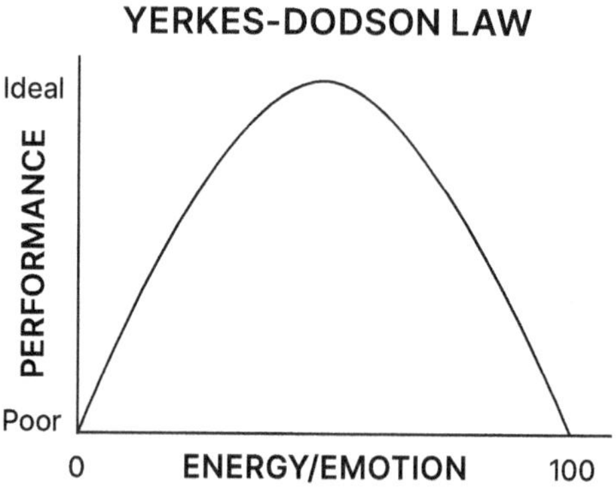

On the left side of the curve, performance suffers when you have too little emotion or energy, such as when you're tired, bored, distracted, or unmotivated. On the right side, performance drops when emotions grow too intense. The top of the curve is where you want to be.

Most golfers try to control emotions only after performance suffers. By then, it's often too late—the mental systems responsible for control are already compromised. You must intervene while emotions are still low-level or rising, or you'll fight uphill to regain balance. While emotions have the upper hand, proper technique gives you control.

Technique to Win the Battle

This technique has four steps. They take longer to explain than to use. With practice, you'll apply them in seconds on the course.

STEP 1: Recognize Early Signs of Emotion

You can't stop what you don't see. Learn your early warning signs and act before emotion escalates. If missed short putts usually trigger frustration, intervene after the first miss. Early action can prevent the emotion from fully forming. Otherwise, you're bringing a water pistol to a gunfight.

STEP 2: Disrupt Momentum

Emotional reactions have momentum. Your job is to interrupt it. Create separation from the emotion, preparing your mind for the correction you'll apply next. Take a diaphragmatic breath. Write a brief note on your scorecard. Use visualization or distraction. What matters isn't the method—it's consistency.

STEP 3: Inject Logic

Your mind is both the tool for emotional control and the first thing weakened by emotion. Injecting logic restores balance.

Create a short phrase or sentence that challenges your reaction. Write it down. Review it before rounds. With repetition, it immediately reduces emotional intensity and eventually prevents emotions from being triggered altogether.

This is like chopping down a tree. You don't get a chainsaw. You get an ax. Over time, you get stronger, the ax gets sharper, and the emotion is reduced to a manageable size. We often think the mind works differently than the body. It doesn't. Strength comes from repetition, just like the swing.

Here are a few examples:

"C-game is where command is built."

"Don't get ahead of yourself, there are more 'its' to find."

"Mistakes happen—snowballing is optional."

"Embrace the challenge and you guarantee improvement."

Injecting Logic works best in your own language. Have one phrase for each of the problems plaguing your game. Write it down rather than relying on memory, which often fails when your mind malfunctions. Train it deliberately—cementing the idea deeply in your mind creates its potency. Even a small reduction in emotion is progress. The excess is unlikely to disappear right away. Keep swinging the ax.

STEP 4: Use a Technical Reminder

The first three steps stabilize emotion, but recovery isn't guaranteed. The game moves quickly. A technical reminder speeds the return to solid execution.

If anger makes you swing harder, focus on grip pressure or tempo.

If pressure ruins speed control, narrow your attention to rhythm.

Write down these keys to your game or swing alongside your Injecting Logic statement so you're not relying on memory.

TECHNIQUE FOR CONTROLLING EMOTIONS

STEP 1 → **STEP 2** → **STEP 3** → **STEP 4**
Recognize   Disrupt   Inject   Technical
Early Signs   Momentum   Logic   Reminder

This technique builds mental strength over time. I define mental strength as how deeply an idea or belief is embedded in your mind.

The strongest performers—elite athletes, military units, great competitors—are grounded in core ideas they trust under pressure. A deeply religious person draws strength from doctrine they believe in. U.S. Navy SEALs live by a creed that begins, "If knocked down, I will get back up, every time," anchoring their actions when fear and chaos are highest. Elite golfers who believe they can win—no matter the circumstances—draw on that same depth of conviction. Their mental strength comes from ideas that hold when emotion threatens to overwhelm everything else.

Train this technique at home, in the car, or on the range. The more you practice, the faster you'll apply it during a round. You won't master it instantly, and sometimes emotions will win. That's part of learning.

Eventually, the right perspective becomes automatic. What once triggered fear, anger, or impatience no longer does. Your emotions aren't gone. You're not an emotionless robot. You've just removed the excess, leaving you full of stable, productive emotion: confidence, motivation, patience. A recipe for quality golf.

Now let's take aim at the most common problems affecting your game.

KEY TAKEAWAYS

Emotion is an essential ingredient to quality golf. But too much of it causes problems, shutting down your ability to think and make decisions.

Intense emotions block your ability to control your emotions. You must start trying to gain control when they're small, otherwise you're in a losing battle.

Injecting Logic trains the right perspective and strengthens your mind to battle excessive emotion. Practice so you're ready.

CORRECTING COMMON PROBLEMS

CHAPTER 7

Leaving Your Game at the Range

"But there is a difference between playing well and hitting the ball well. Hitting the ball well is about thirty percent of it. The rest is being comfortable with the different situations on the course."

— MICKEY WRIGHT

You arrive at the course early and hit the range, optimistic about what lies ahead. Your first wedge shot—a crisp, pure strike—lifts your confidence. As you work through the bag, making effortless swings with your irons and woods, each one confirms the promise of a great round ahead. You're dialed in. Ready to go.

You enjoy the walk to the first tee, laughing with your playing partners, soaking in the moment. And then the magic disappears. A snap hook off the first tee. A thinned approach over the green. A chunked chip. A three-putt from 15 feet. Shell-shocked, you walk off the first green wondering what just happened.

This isn't the first time you've had a great warmup only to lose it on the course. Even when the momentum carries into the early holes, once it fades you often find it difficult, if not impossible, to get your game back without returning to the comfort of the practice tee.

Why does this happen? Why do you become such a different player on the course, hitting shots you would never hit on the range? How does a rhythmic, free-flowing swing turn tense and choppy? Why do you stub and skull chips after making clean contact moments earlier? How can your pace on the greens go awry so quickly?

Given how common this complaint is, you've likely tried to make sense of it. It's just as puzzling when the opposite happens—when you hit it poorly on the range and then play great. This disconnect proves an important point: What you do before the round can influence your chances of playing well, but it does not determine how you'll play. What has a far greater impact is your mentality. Understanding how your warmup affects your mindset can help you play better golf.

A terrible range session can actually help you find the right frame of mind by removing the burden of overconfidence and unrealistic expectations. That's often why you play better. With confidence lowered, you swing a little easier, choose more conservative targets, avoid big mistakes, and recover more calmly from poor shots. You adopt a "let's go see what I can do" mindset, and your attention sharpens.

Conversely, when you flush it on the range, your confidence can rise too high. That confidence often turns into expectation, and expectation leaves you less prepared for the reality of the game. This isn't a suggestion to hit it poorly on purpose. The key is staying realistic about your game and resisting the illusion created by a great warmup.

That illusion comes from mistaking the practice environment for the golf course. They are fundamentally different. On the range, there are no consequences. You can hit a massive slice or blow a putt five feet past the hole and immediately hit another ball, erasing the miss from memory—a luxury unavailable on the course. Practice areas offer flat, predictable lies, or artificial turf, rather than the uneven stances and awkward slopes found on the course. You can hit the same shot repeatedly, building momentum that can never be replicated during a round. You're on your own schedule, free from the pressure of being ready when it's your turn. And you're usually more energized during warmup than you'll be on the back nine.

When you make consistent contact and feel great warming up, it can be enjoyable. But it's important to recognize the false confidence created in an artificial setting.

What changes on the course isn't your swing; it's the situation. Golf is a dynamic game that demands adaptation. It has consequences. Every shot counts, time matters, and myriad factors compete for your attention. You're thinking about score, hazards, wind, your playing partners, and what the last shot might mean for the next one. That added cognitive load fractures focus and exposes weaknesses that never appear in practice.

A great warmup can leave you less prepared to handle adversity, manage expectations, and respond to inevitable swings in performance. You don't need confidence to play well. You need access to your skills, your knowledge, and your experience. The rounds where you played well despite low confidence are proof of this. Too much confidence, however, adds pressure, reduces focus, and leads to frustration and disappointment. Those conditions make good golf harder, not easier.

The game you see on the course is your real game. Not the range session. Not the practice green. Your real game lives in the bell curve of your last 40-plus rounds—the full range of outcomes you actually produce. If you're a 10-handicap, that curve includes doubles, missed greens, and imperfect swings, even on good days. A great warmup offers a glimpse of future potential, a peek toward the front edge of that curve. It shows what might be possible one day with time and development.

It would be nice if you could simply copy and paste those shots to the course, but golf doesn't work that way. Improvement doesn't arrive all at once; it creeps forward as the curve slowly shifts. Understanding where you are on that curve—your true baseline—is what allows you to shift it forward. When you accept your current range of outcomes, you stop fighting reality and start working with it. You make smarter decisions, manage your emotions better, and create the conditions for actual improvement. That's why your mind goes into a tailspin when you hit shots on the course you would never hit on the range. Reality reasserts itself and catches you off guard.

I'm not trying to get you down. I'm trying to give you the clearest path forward. What actually helps you play better golf is accepting where you are right now so you can make the decisions that move you forward: realism, adaptability, and restraint. That starts with rethinking how you warm up.

Better Warm-Up Strategies

A good warmup is defined by what prepares you to play well that day, not what makes you feel best in the moment. A reliable approach is aiming for your B-game, which includes parts of your game that are dependable but still require intention and discipline.

Reinforcing your B-game gives you a stronger foundation from which you can earn your A-game on the course. For example, you might focus on fundamentals like posture, alignment, and tempo. You can assess how your body feels to decide whether to swing aggressively or rely on three-quarter shots for control. You might rehearse your pre-shot routine, practice committing to decisions, or focus on starting the ball on a specific line. These are skills that transfer directly to the course.

There's no one-size-fits-all approach. Golfers are a mixed bunch. The right warmup is the one that consistently leads to better decisions and calmer reactions once you're keeping score. If you're not sure what that is, experiment. Over your next several rounds, try different approaches and look for patterns—not in how well you warm up, but in how well you play.

Here are a few ideas:

Don't Hit Balls

Get your body ready by stretching, activating key golf muscles, or whatever you need physically, but skip the range entirely. This may cost you a shot or two early, but it forces you to adapt on the course rather than rely on artificial momentum. And it makes your mentality and swing more reliable. This approach is especially useful if you tend to rush, hit a dozen balls, and sprint to the first tee. Starting relaxed often does more for tempo than a perfect warmup.

Mix It Up

Don't hit the same shot repeatedly. That doesn't happen on the course unless you've hit it out of bounds. Instead, space your shots out. Chat, reset, then hit the next ball with intention. Or never hit the same club twice. Change targets, trajectories, or shot shapes. If you do hit the same club, vary the target and distance. Occasionally go through your full pre-shot routine. The goal is to prepare for the variability you'll face on the course, not build false confidence through repetition. This is particularly important on the practice green if you struggle with speed control or short putts.

Use Proven Adjustments

If you're not hitting it well, don't start searching for a new swing thought or a magical feel. You're unlikely to find something reliable minutes before a round. Instead, lean on adjustments you already trust. If you don't have any, that's a good reason to take a lesson—not to overhaul your swing, but to identify simple, repeatable fixes like alignment, ball position, or setup. The goal is a troubleshooting plan for your current swing, not a rebuild.

Regardless of the strategy you choose, don't keep hitting balls just to leave on a high note. If you tell yourself a shot is your last one, be true to your word. That small dose of pressure is useful. Treat it like the opening tee shot. If it doesn't go well, remind yourself that the mentality you bring to the course matters more than how the ball behaved on the range. Bad warmups don't cause bad rounds. They create opportunities to practice resilience.

In the end, your goal isn't to take your game from the range to the course. It's to play better golf. Bringing the right mentality to your warmup increases your chances.

When it comes to making swing changes, things are different. Then, you are trying to take something from the range to the course. That process requires patience, trust, and a clear plan for transfer. We'll address those topics next.

KEY TAKEAWAYS

The practice environment is not golf. Don't allow a great warmup to give you false confidence. Be prepared to handle adversity and the inevitable ups and downs.

A good warmup is the one that prepares you to play well and gets you in the right state of mind. If you're not sure what that is, experiment.

Bad warmups don't cause bad rounds. They're opportunities to practice resilience.

CHAPTER 8

When Practice Doesn't Translate to the Course

"Your final goal is to convert your athletic swing to pure instinct rather than conscious thought."

— DAVID LEADBETTER

You're doing everything right. Grinding at the range, repeating putting drills, working with a pro. Maybe you've bought the latest training aid, picked up a useful tip from a better player, or studied video of your swing frame by frame.

Your dedication is paying off. You're striping it on the range and draining everything on the putting green. You wrap up your practice session feeling dialed in.

Then you hit the course and *bam*! Your old habits return. You stop trusting your new takeaway. Your new shoulder alignment no longer feels right. You can't remember how much wrist hinge you need on a 40-yard pitch. It's a brutal betrayal, made worse when you think of all the hours you've invested. Meanwhile, your friend who hasn't practiced in months cards a cool 76. You leave the course frustrated, demotivated, and confused.

What the heck just happened? The problem is related to the warmup issue we discussed in the last chapter, but it runs even deeper. When you groove something on the range, you're building confidence that isn't entirely earned. To recognize that is to be realistic, which is healthy. But understanding why practice doesn't transfer—and how to fix it—involves more than adjusting your expectations. It requires some theory.

The Transfer Problem

Ideally, you want changes in your swing to become automatic. No swing thoughts, no mechanics—just play. In the Adult Learning Model from Chapter 4, that's Unconscious Competence. The technique is mastered and shows up without conscious effort.

Here's the catch: Mastering something on the driving range doesn't mean it's mastered on the course. Learning is context-specific. As situations get more challenging—more consequence, more pressure, different conditions—you need more skill to meet the demand.

Think about your last lesson. Under the instructor's watchful eye, you hit it better than ever. The next day on the range, you can't recreate it. So you take another lesson. This time it clicks. Back on the range, you can reproduce the change consistently, but only with your short irons. It takes a few more range sessions before it works with your woods.

Each step up requires more reps, more mastery. A lesson is easier than solo block practice. Block practice is easier than the course, which represents a much bigger jump than most golfers realize.

Here's how the challenge escalates:

- Lesson with an instructor
- Block practice on the range
- Randomized practice
- Casual round on an easy course
- Money match or club event

- Tournament on a tough course

- Tournament with a chance to win

Your personal order might vary—maybe money matches sharpen your focus—but the principle holds. As difficulty increases, you need more skill. That's why expecting block practice to translate seamlessly to a Sunday Nassau is like expecting to jump from a step stool to the roof.

Sure, momentum might carry you for a few holes. You'll get a false sense that you've cracked it. But when that fades, your response matters. Don't panic and search for something new. Remember you're in a learning process that needs time. The transfer has begun, but you'll need *many, many* more reps before it's locked in. Until then, you risk reverting to old habits.

Use the Adult Learning Model as a gauge. If you need swing thoughts, drills, or rehearsal swings to execute, you're at Conscious Competence. If those don't work, you're at Conscious Incompetence—you know what to do but can't do it yet. Sometimes you'll slip all the way back to Unconscious Incompetence, where you forget the change entirely. Track these stages as you move through tougher situations.

In theory, you should progress methodically: block practice to drill technique, then randomize targets with time between shots, then play a few holes. But that's not practical for most golfers, and it's not required. You can jump straight from the range to a money match—just keep the Adult Learning Model in mind so your expectations stay realistic. Even if you play great immediately, you'll still need more reps to truly reach Unconscious Competence.

This perspective protects you from overconfidence. It also reminds you that you might backslide. You won't assume improvements will automatically appear when stakes rise. Instead, your confidence is based on what shows up under fire. Stay optimistic and focused on making the transfer over many rounds, and those changes will gradually become permanent.

Unless you hit a roadblock. What if you lose trust in the changes you've been trying to implement? What then?

Breaking the Trust Barrier

A lack of trust paralyzes progress. You might be standing in your own way, turning the bridge from range to course into a leap of faith you're not willing to take.

Old habits die hard. You know the new move works better, but over the ball—with water left and O.B. right—you instinctively revert to what feels comfortable. And the new swing doesn't.

Remember, change feels uncomfortable because it is. It's not natural to you, like the old, familiar pattern. Discomfort is inevitable. How you interpret it is what matters. Most players treat discomfort as a signal that something's wrong. It's the opposite. Discomfort with a new move is proof you're doing something right. Embrace it. Get the reps that make your swing better, even at the risk of hitting poor shots.

Lack of trust can also be a form of unhealthy self-protection. You're trying to shield your confidence from a devastating hit. Rather than risk an embarrassing triple that invalidates all your practice, you retreat to your old swing, hoping you can log enough range time to make the transfer happen magically. Then you won't need trust—the change will just be there.

But hiding on the range only makes the problem worse. It requires an even bigger leap and more trust when you finally face consequences. You need to risk poor outcomes on the course now, because extreme caution is a greater long-term threat. Protecting against the downside prevents you from realizing any upside.

Yes, bringing improvements to demanding situations might get messy. But you do this to play better golf in the future. Investments can't be realized by protecting yourself from pain, discomfort, or triples.

Give yourself permission to stumble. That doesn't mean it will happen—freeing yourself from unrealistic expectations might be exactly what lets you succeed. Bring your focus and athleticism and see what you've got. It's fine if changes only last a few holes or show up sporadically. You already knew more reps were needed. Now you know something's starting to stick. Plus, you'll learn what helps you progress. It might be a clearer swing thought or different process.

Being aware of how the Adult Learning Model applies to technical changes will help you stay patient and less frustrated, so you can stick with the learning process longer.

If you still can't make practice translate after giving this a real shot, you may be dealing with other problems I cover in this book. Most commonly: overthinking technique and trying to work on too many things at once. I'll tackle both in the next chapter.

KEY TAKEAWAYS

To thrive in more challenging situations, you need context-specific skills you can't get from practice.

Use the Adult Learning Model to measure progress and remind you that steps backward are still possible as you make the transfer.

Protecting yourself from pain and big numbers makes them more likely. Giving yourself room to stumble allows you to succeed.

CHAPTER 9

Overthinking Technique

"You swing your best when you have the
fewest things to think about."
— BOBBY JONES

Golf is a physical sport best played in an athletic, reactive way that blends technique with a feel for the shot at hand. You don't need to consider yourself an athlete to play like that. Some of you are natural athletes, but athleticism can also be developed through practice and play.

Think about the good golf shots you've hit without the benefit of a perfect swing. Maybe your path drifted too far inside on the downswing and your hands rotated faster to square the clubface at impact. That wasn't luck. That was a deeply ingrained skill adapting in real time. That's athleticism.

The problem is, you can't adapt—or play athletically—when your mind is cluttered with swing thoughts.

Overthinking technique requires too much focus and pulls your attention away from what the golf course is asking of you. If this only happened occasionally, it wouldn't be a serious concern. But many golfers have become so reliant on their mind to swing the club that they've trapped themselves in a cycle and can't escape.

Constant tinkering—searching for a swing thought that will always work—makes your swing less reliable, not more. You plug leaks temporarily, but after a few bad shots (which everyone hits), a frantic search begins for the next fix. Rinse. Repeat. You're stuck.

This vicious cycle shows up at every level of the game, though it isn't always obvious. See if any of these sound familiar:

- You're always working on something, but changes don't stick and your ball-striking wavers between hot and cold

- Slight misses lead you to sift through swing thoughts mid-round until your head feels jumbled

- Using swing thoughts over the ball is so ingrained you can't imagine hitting a shot without them

- Taking lessons makes it hard to play without hyper-focusing on mechanics

- You scrutinize great shots as closely as bad ones, trying to reverse-engineer perfection

If you see yourself here, you're not broken—and you're not alone.

Why Thinking So Much Backfires

Imagine thinking about how you walk the same way you think about your swing.

"Lift foot. Rotate hips. Extend knee. Plant heel." Try it; you'll feel how walking becomes awkward when you attempt to control it consciously.

The golf swing is more complex than placing one foot in front of the other, and it does require technical work. But the same principle applies: You can't swing naturally when you're overly dependent on your conscious mind.

Many of you already know you're too "in your head," but you haven't been able to get out of it. The reason your game feels stuck is that relying on swing thoughts actually blocks learning. Your base of skill stops growing because you're stuck at the Conscious Competence stage, where improvements require constant mental supervision.

The problem is, the mind isn't very good at supervising fast, complex movements.

A golf swing moves the clubhead at 90-plus miles per hour and unfolds in less than a second and a half. Trying to consciously control that motion is like using your lower back to lift heavy furniture. Those muscles weren't designed for the job. That's why you have glutes, quads, and hamstrings.

Your mind isn't designed to control your swing either. It's designed to train it.

Real control comes from what you've trained to Unconscious Competence, where improvements are so deeply ingrained that thinking is no longer required. When you reach that level, your mind naturally quiets down. When you use your legs properly, your back stops barking. Same idea.

What the Mind Is Good For

One reason the mind struggles to control the swing is that it's limited in size.

Working memory—the part of the brain where the voice in your head lives—is often compared to a whiteboard. It's where you consciously hold information, make decisions, and direct attention. Under normal conditions, that whiteboard can hold somewhere between five and nine pieces of information.[4]

Ideally, over the ball, your entire whiteboard is devoted to the shot: target, trajectory, distance, intention. Behind the ball, using one piece of that space for a swing thought or feel is perfectly fine.

Here's the catch: When emotions run high or energy drops low, the whiteboard shrinks.

Think back to a time you made double bogey on an easy hole. On the next tee, the whiteboard isn't clean—smudges remain. You're frustrated and still replaying mistakes, leaving less space to read the wind, commit to a club, or connect to the shot. That's not a personal flaw. It's human nature.

This limitation is a law, not a preference. We don't get to override it; we have to work within it.

That's why the strength of your connection to a swing thought matters. If that connection is weak, it won't show up when pressure rises. A swing thought that works on the range disappears when you tee it up because the added challenge of playing weakens your connection to it. This is the same principle behind Injecting Logic, the technique discussed in Chapter 6. A thought only helps if it's been trained deeply enough to survive emotional interference.

Many swing thoughts don't fail. You abandon them before they're fully integrated.

Using Swing Thoughts the Right Way

This chapter isn't about thinking less. It's about thinking at the right time.

Used properly, swing thoughts are scaffolding. They help support change—the new structure you're building—and then fade into the background. The goal is to move from consciously managing your swing to unconsciously swinging it better than before.

As I mentioned in the last chapter, you develop real control by better sequencing improvements in your swing.

On the course, that means limiting yourself to one swing thought, or feel, and only to something that's already familiar. If a change isn't well-trained, the course isn't the place to force it.

This is where instructors can be invaluable. Build your swing in the right order, and when you move on to the next piece, the earlier ones remain available if things start to slip.

Give yourself time. The urge to pile on swing thoughts won't disappear overnight. You've played golf that way for years. Changing how you use your mind isn't easy, and is often uncomfortable, especially when your swing falters and instinct screams for a quick fix.

Quick fixes got you here. Permanent upgrades take patience and steady progress.

The Do's and Don'ts of Swing Thoughts

Here are a few additional ideas on how to use swing thoughts more effectively:

Don't Use Them Over the Ball

Using a swing thought over the ball is like taking an open-book test. You never truly learn the material. Over the ball, your job is to remain committed to the shot. Ideally, you're reacting freely, or you've already used your one thought during a rehearsal swing. Your mind may drift toward mechanics, but gently redirect it back to the target. Over time, trust builds.

Don't Look for Perfect

There's always something to improve, but chasing "it" trains your mind to hunt endlessly. The goal isn't mythical perfection. It's the next small step. There's *always* a next step, no matter how good you are. For now, though, you don't have to keep working on more and more stuff. Improving your golf swing takes time and effort. Sometimes the most effective move is to stop upgrading and start playing.

Do Gauge Your Progress

When changing your swing, test how well it holds up under pressure and demanding situations. Occasionally, you may integrate multiple changes successfully. Other times, one falls apart. That's feedback. It's not a cue to search for something new. It simply shows what needs more training.

Relinquishing mental control is easier on the range than on the course. On the course, free your mind by shifting attention outward—to the target, the shot shape, the task. Give your training a chance to show up.

The transfer takes time. Expect some turbulence, especially in difficult conditions or high-pressure moments. Progress isn't linear, but the trend matters.

As much as swing thoughts can crowd your mind, score can crowd it too. The running tally has a way of sneaking in, draining enjoyment, and costing strokes. That's where we're headed next.

KEY TAKEAWAYS

Relying on swing thoughts blocks you from playing golf in an athletic, reactive way.

Your mind is designed to help train your swing, not control it.

Building your swing in the right order develops real control. Stick with one swing thought long enough to fully integrate it.

CHAPTER 10

Ruled By Score

"I kept telling myself this word:
process. Focus on my process,
don't care about the result."

— RORY MCILROY

"What'd you shoot?" It's the question we typically get asked in the grill room after a round. It reflects an obvious truth about golf: Score matters, and it's a primary reason you want to improve.

You want to shoot lower scores, reduce your handicap, beat your friends, and win tournaments. But when score dominates your mind during the round, you often play worse and post higher scores. We can't deny or shy away from the reality that score matters, so something has to change.

Part of you already knows you focus too much on score. You've tried to put it out of your mind, but the internal calculator doesn't stop. You always know where you stand relative to par or a target score for the day. This is especially true when you get off to a bad start. Trying harder to make up ground only makes things worse—confidence drops, frustration rises, nerves fray.

Even when you just want to have fun and escape the daily grind, score stays at the forefront of your mind. You dwell on missed opportunities, berate yourself for a careless three-putt, and dread the blow-up hole that could send the round off the rails.

When it comes to score, the mind loves to jump into the future by adding up what you need to do to break 80, shoot your handicap, or avoid an embarrassing number. This counter-productive math problem is hard to shut off, especially when a great front nine dangles a career-best and you start envisioning the tougher holes on the back nine with a mix of excitement and nervous anticipation. Tension ratchets up as the round progresses, and score takes up more anxious space in your mind. Playing well should be fun and energizing, yet low scores are often rattling and can trip you up down the stretch.

Then there's the opposite experience. After a terrible front nine, you stop caring and play much better on the back, as if someone body-snatched you at the turn. After the round, you chalk it up to golf being a crazy game. But it's not random. It's a clear sign that you play better when you're less emotionally tied to score. Of course, "not caring about score" isn't in your nature, which is why that approach doesn't work as a strategy.

Standard-issue advice hasn't worked either. You've tried to stay in the present, ignore results, take it one shot at a time, have fun, not let bad holes get to you, and remember it's only a game. These platitudes sound good, but they rarely make a dent in your hard-driving focus on score.

They fall short because your emphasis on score produces more emotion than you realize.

Whether it's frustration or despair when you underperform, or anxiety and excitement when you play well, emotions escalate and bleed into the next shot, the next hole, or even the next round. Remember the Yerkes-Dodson Law from Chapter 6: You play your best when you find the right balance of energy and emotion to keep you near the top of the curve.

Some players thrive by focusing on score. Knowing where they stand throughout the round or in a match helps sustain focus and competitiveness. But for most golfers, dwelling on score triggers too much emotion and sends them tumbling down the right side of the performance curve. Do any of the following statements apply to you?

- You expect to play better, and high scores drive you nuts

- You become nervous and don't want to mess up a chance for a low score

- You want all the time and energy spent trying to improve to pay off

- You need proof you can compete with better players

- You badly want to play to your potential and hate playing poorly

- You tie too much confidence to score and feel down about yourself after bad rounds

While these may seem unrelated, they share a common thread. You're using score alone to judge how well you're playing. That gives you an incomplete, and often misleading, picture. Some players are so accustomed to evaluating their game by score that they don't recognize when they're actually playing well. They lose sight of the fact that their number is inflated by a couple of poor decisions or small misses that were excessively punished.

To focus less on score—and produce better scores over time—you need feedback that looks beyond the number.

Score Doesn't Tell the Whole Truth

When you rely only on score to judge performance, you're effectively saying that your play equals your score. That perspective is incomplete. You can't tell what role luck played, or what you did well or poorly, just by looking at the card. There's a reason we say there are no pictures on the scorecard: it's true.

As every golfer knows, you can hit a poor shot that turns out fine on one hole and hit a decent shot on the next that settles right behind a tree. You can make a great swing or roll a putt exactly as intended and still get the wrong result, like flushing a 3-wood that lands just over the green, bounces into a hazard, and leads to a difficult up-and-down you don't convert. A beautifully struck shot costs you three strokes, while a more average swing on the previous hole left you a tap-in.

Of course, you want control over the scores you shoot. But when score is the only feedback your mind receives, the only apparent solution becomes trying to control score by thinking about score. That's the trap. And it helps explain why this problem has been so hard to solve.

The way to gain more control over your scoring is by shifting your focus to two elements: your process and your ability to recognize luck. Together, they give your mind better feedback and reduce its fixation on score. The formula is simple:

YOUR PROCESS + LUCK = SCORE

Technical skill also belongs in this equation, since it strongly influences scoring. But given the scope of this book—and the fact that many golfers who obsess over score also overthink technique—we'll leave it aside here.

Luck is an inherent part of the game, yet many players struggle to spot it. Your score in a given round can easily vary by five shots or more based on the breaks you do or don't get. While you can't control luck, recognizing its influence is an important skill. When that skill is weak, you'll overestimate or underestimate your own play, which fuels emotion and erodes composure. Spotting bad luck comes easily; noticing good luck is much harder. We'll dig into that more in the next chapter.

Understanding what you control in your process can be confusing given the game's complexity. Generally, it includes shot selection, commitment to decisions, focus, emotional stability, energy level, awareness of course conditions, and the ability to adjust as your game changes. Players with better technical skills often have more refined processes as well, such as picking precise targets, judging ball flight and spin out of the rough, and reducing tension in their swing.

A quality process isn't guaranteed, especially when your mind defaults to score. When that happens, redirect your attention to something process-related you can improve, even slightly, such as adapting decisions to your shot pattern for the day, committing fully to a choice, or interrupting negative thoughts. Each small redirect retrains your mind to see process as something you control.

Emphasizing process is especially important when you're on pace for a career day. Focusing on what you need to shoot over the remaining holes is, at best, a distraction. Your score on the first 14 holes has zero impact on what you'll shoot on the last four. You can't carry pars or birdies forward. What you do bring with you is your process. The stronger it is, the better you'll handle pressure, and the more likely you'll finish the round with a good story to tell.

Another reason score holds such power is that you're asking it to prove something it can't. A low round doesn't permanently raise your A-game, just as a high score doesn't eliminate it. Your bell curve is a far better predictor of your golf than any single number. The potential for a bad round is roughly the same after a great one, and a poor round doesn't reduce your chances of shooting low the next time out.

When you forget this, your emotions become tightly bound to score. Process is where your control actually lives.

After the round, reinforce that emphasis by taking a few minutes to informally grade your non-scoring elements. Ask yourself questions like:

- How was the quality of my decisions?

- Was I fully committed to those decisions?

- What was my level of focus before and during each shot?

- How well did I judge course conditions and adapt to changes?

- Was I able to adjust to changes in my physical, mental, or emotional state?

- Where did I get lucky or unlucky?

These questions help separate what you controlled from what you didn't and balance your perspective on the round. They also tend to reveal patterns—both strengths and weaknesses— that score alone hides.

You could score your process during or after the round. Mental scorecards exist for this purpose, but many players struggle to stick with them long enough to gain value. That's fine. The goal is simply to establish a baseline, decide what most needs improvement, and notice progress over time. You don't need to do this if your only goal is to loosen your grip on score.

A- to C-Game Analysis

If you want to grade your process more precisely and make meaningful improvements, I recommend a tool I call an A- to C-Game Analysis. It builds on the bell curve concept from Chapter 2 and creates an objective measure of your A-, B-, and C-game processes. You can do the same for your technical skills as well. Here's a sample to give you a sense of what it looks like:

A- TO C-GAME ANALYSIS

C–GAME	B–GAME	A–GAME
DECISIONS		
Only focused on distance, don't think about wind direction or how the ball will react on the ground.	Forget to select a specific target, defaulting to a general area.	Easily analyze the situation and consider important factors, including my gut.
COMMITMENT		
Mostly an issue in putting, where I change the read over the ball, second-guess it, and still hit it.	Less committed when faced with an unusual lie or when I want to be too aggressive but still hit the shot anyway.	Happens easily. No doubts about the right shot to hit or the line I've selected putting, even in tough situations.

C–GAME	B–GAME	A–GAME
FOCUS		
Thinking too much about things outside of golf. Mind is all over the place. Hitting shots on autopilot.	Connection to the shot is weaker. I'm thinking too much about score or get caught up in conversation.	Full connection to the shot, not even random noises can distract me.
EMOTION		
Overconfident and being way too aggressive. Frustrated by how badly I'm hitting it and can't figure out why.	Unsure of what's happening in my swing. Lack the confidence to swing hard. Little things are irritating.	Confident. Enjoying the round. Things that are normally frustrating, don't bother me at all.
ENERGY		
Energy lags so much that I can't will myself to try harder. Too tired to be frustrated about it. Mind goes totally blank at times.	Have moments where my mind will short out but can recover quickly.	Feeling great!
AWARENESS		
Not tuned in. Ignoring obvious factors. Forcing stock yardages.	Focused only on what's obvious, making standard reads of lies or course conditions.	Seeing subtleties in the green. Good feel for how hard to swing and how far the ball is going without any tech.

To create your own, start by brainstorming how your decisions, commitment, focus, emotions, energy, and awareness vary. The extremes are usually easiest to identify, so begin with the best and worst versions of each element, then fill in your B-game.

Create a draft before your next round. Afterwards, answer the reflection questions in the previous list and revise based on what you notice. Continue refining until the differences between your A-, B-, and C-game feel clear and stable.

This tool allows you to grade your process more accurately, which helps free your mind from obsessing over score. Most players never intentionally develop their process, even though it's far easier than making major swing changes.

The final piece of the equation—luck—can't be controlled. But your ability to recognize it can dramatically improve your emotional balance and perspective. Most golfers struggle with this, which is why we'll dig into it next.

KEY TAKEAWAYS

Let's normalize asking "How'd you play?" with an emphasis on process, not just score.

Focusing on process doesn't change your aspirations for low scores; it gives you better feedback to achieve them.

Grading your process helps free your mind from being ruled by score.

CHAPTER 11

Overreacting to Bad Breaks

"Life is not fair, so why should I make a course that is fair?"
— PETE DYE

You know that luck is part of the game. Golf is played outdoors on imperfect surfaces, under unpredictable conditions, with fine margins separating success from failure. Some days, the breaks just don't go your way.

You try to accept this. You tell yourself to be patient, remind yourself that this is golf, and attempt to move on. But knowing this intellectually and managing it emotionally are two very different things. When your best drive of the day ends up in a divot, your ball is stymied behind a lone tree just off the fairway, or a putt lips out, it's hard not to feel angry, cheated, or pessimistic. That reaction often shows up immediately: You rush your next shot, get overly aggressive with a recovery, or try to ram a five-foot putt into the back of the hole.

Occasionally, that frustration works in your favor. Motivation comes in many forms. More often, though, it produces another poor outcome and your anger compounds. Now you're frustrated and annoyed with yourself for letting a routine dose of bad luck cost you additional shots. You let the rub of the green get under your skin, and it's hurting your score. This is a problem worth addressing.

Costly reactions to bad luck extend beyond individual shots to the way you view luck in the game as a whole. Common examples include:

- Believing you get more bad breaks than other players

- Deciding, at some point, that you're simply "unlucky"

- Feeling like the course owes you something, preferably immediately

- Complaining after the round about what you would have shot

- Expecting bad breaks before they happen

- Losing motivation to practice because "what's the point?"

We're born with a strong desire for fairness, a tendency observable even in infants.[5] This hardwired sense of justice makes bad breaks feel personal, even when they're entirely random. Not every golfer overreacts to bad luck, however, which means the issue is not the breaks themselves but how they're interpreted.

You may believe that you receive more than your fair share of bad breaks compared to others. Yet the fact that you play enough golf to care about improving suggests you're already fairly fortunate. You're reading a book about golf, after all. Have you factored that into your perception of good luck?

I'm not suggesting that gratitude alone will prevent emotional reactions on the course. The point is simpler: Golfers tend to view luck in an unbalanced way.

Players remember bad luck far more vividly than good luck. Bad breaks evoke stronger emotional responses than even extremely fortunate outcomes. As a result, you're far more likely to dwell on poor lies, lip-outs, or distractions in your backswing than on favorable bounces or perfect lies in the rough. Over time, this pattern repeats itself and becomes ingrained.

That imbalance makes you react more negatively to bad luck in the present. Put another way, you've become highly skilled at spotting bad luck and remarkably poor at noticing good luck. These reactions are intensified further when you make two common attribution errors:

- Assuming good luck is the result of your skill
- Blaming poor execution on bad luck, which conveniently removes responsibility

Taken together, these tendencies tip the scales of golfing justice. It becomes reasonable, at least in your own mind, to conclude that you're unlucky, that the course owes you, or that the game is unfair. This is especially true when you're struggling or under pressure. Added emotion erases logic, and bad luck is all you remember. Saying "I can't catch a break" feels accurate in that moment because you truly believe it.

Figures 1 and 2 illustrate how this imbalance develops.

Figure 1

Figure 1 represents an ideal perspective. The scale reflects luck, with good luck on the right and bad luck on the left.

Beneath the scale are two piles: "Skills," representing positive execution, or your A-game; and "Mistakes," representing poor execution, or your B- and C-game.

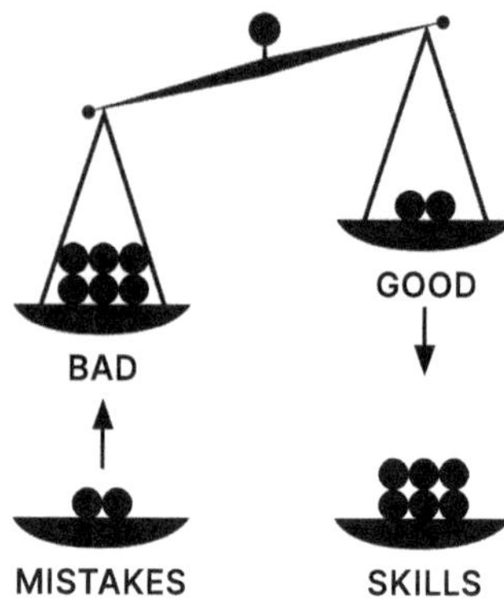

Figure 2

Figure 2 shows how this perspective becomes distorted. When you hit a decent shot that receives a favorable bounce and finishes better than expected, but you credit the outcome entirely to your ability, good luck is removed from the scale and added to the skills pile. In your mind, you didn't get lucky; you hit a quality shot. Naturally.

Like when you hit an approach shot slightly thin into an elevated green with the pin cut in front. The ball catches the slope short of the putting surface and trickles up to eight feet. Good fortune has shined on you. Even a well-struck shot likely would have finished 25 feet away.

On the other hand, when a poor shot produces a bad outcome and you attribute the result to bad luck, mistakes are transferred onto the scale as misfortune. Using the same example, if that thinned approach carries a few yards farther, lands on the front edge, and rolls over the back of the green, you're left with a difficult up-and-down. Now the story becomes one of bad luck.

By crediting good luck to skill and blaming mistakes on luck, it becomes easy to conclude that you're unlucky. This belief is reinforced during periods of poor play or pressure, when emotion overwhelms perspective and negative outcomes dominate your memory.

Expecting bad luck only intensifies this reaction. Predicting misfortune is common when you're struggling, especially after a stretch of poor lies or missed putts. Some golfers go further and develop superstitions: lucky balls, unlucky holes, or rituals meant to ward off trouble.

Superstitions aren't inherently harmful, but allowing them to shape your expectations is. You don't know what's going to happen. Predicting a bad outcome that then occurs can cause the accumulated frustration of previous rounds to erupt in a momentary loss of control. Cue the club toss.

To be clear, feeling frustrated by bad breaks is natural. The problem is not the initial emotional response; it's how that reaction compounds and distorts decision-making on subsequent shots.

There's another subtle consequence. When the outcome you predicted actually happens, such as when your tee shot ends up blocked just as you thought, a subconscious belief forms that you really do know what is coming. This exaggerates your sense of control.

You're not psychic.

The control you do have comes from your process: choosing shots that match your capabilities, accounting for wind and conditions, committing fully, and allowing your athleticism to function without excessive swing thoughts. When your attention is fixed on bad luck, it's no longer focused on the details that actually influence shot quality.

An inability to accurately assess luck also contributes to overconfidence. When you already have an inflated sense of skill, mistakes are easily discounted and poor outcomes are readily blamed on misfortune.

Balancing the Scales

This unbalanced perspective has been reinforced over time, which is why well-intended advice only provides temporary relief. To correct it, you must become better at recognizing good luck, a skill most golfers are surprisingly weak at.

Examples of good luck that often go unnoticed include:

- Favorable weather (unless you live in San Diego)

- A fortunate lie in the woods after a poor tee shot

- The ball sitting up nicely in the rough

- Barely missing a water hazard or out-of-bounds

- Watching a playing partner putt on the same line

- A clean bunker lie

- Yardages that allow for a full swing rather than an in-between shot

- A putt hit too firmly that still drops

- Pin locations that suit your preferred ball flight

Given how underdeveloped this skill is, consider marking instances of good luck on your scorecard during the round. It may feel unnatural at first. That's part of the point. Simply look-ing for good luck begins to shift your perspective.

Next, when you believe you were unlucky, pause and ask whether the shot could have been executed better. The goal is not to assign blame but to remain open to the idea that luck is only one variable. Sometimes the answer is clear. A sudden gust of wind knocks down a well-struck shot. Other times, the outcome reflects both factors. You block a tee shot that hits the cart path and shoots out of bounds. The swing was poor, but the result was made worse by circumstance.

As you track good luck and reassess moments you labeled as unlucky, your perspective will gradually become more accurate. It's also useful to note occasions when you predicted a bad out-come that never materialized, allowing you to challenge those assumptions as well.

To accelerate this process, you can review your broader golf history, or even other areas of your life, and identify moments of good fortune you once attributed solely to skill, as well as setbacks better explained by mistakes than misfortune. You cannot change the past, but recalibrating how you view it can stabilize how you respond in the present. Do this after rounds and revisit it regularly rather than treating it as a one-time exercise.

While perspective can shift quickly, reshaping it perma-nently takes time. If progress stalls, part of the resistance may come from a reluctance to admit that good luck plays a role in your best rounds. You want to believe you're good enough to shoot low scores entirely on your own merit. Acknowledging the role of fortune can feel like diminishing achievement, even though luck is as integral to the game as skill.

The golfer who can accurately assess both ability and fortune, celebrating great rounds while acknowledging the breaks that helped along the way, develops a far more accurate view of performance. This balanced perspective reduces frustration and creates a foundation for genuine improvement. When you can see luck clearly, you can finally focus your energy on what you truly control.

Overconfidence, however, does not only distort how you view luck. It undermines your game in subtler and more pervasive ways than most golfers realize. In the next chapter, we will examine how this hidden problem shows up on the course and what you can do about it.

KEY TAKEAWAYS

A skewed memory makes it seem like you're unlucky. Actually, you're just better at recognizing bad luck than good luck.

You can't control luck; you can only control your process. Don't let the rub of the green distract you from the details that influence quality shot-making.

Steadily rebalance your perspective by noting instances of good luck and substandard execution.

CHAPTER 12

Overconfidence

*"Golf is the hardest game in the world. There is
no way you can ever get it. Just when you think you do,
the game jumps up and puts you in your place."*

— BEN CRENSHAW

Overconfidence is one of the most common problems in golf. It's also one of the sneakiest. You likely don't realize that it's costing you strokes, disrupting momentum, and breaking your rhythm.

Overconfidence hides in plain sight because you're constantly told you need confidence. If that's the case, how could it be wrong to feel great over a particular shot or about your game? The problem is there's a fine line between confidence and complacency, not to mention believing something about your ability that isn't true. Because golf doesn't provide perfect feedback, it's easy to develop a distorted sense of reality. This shift can happen quietly, even if you're not being outwardly arrogant or boastful. When this occurs, however, an exaggerated view of skill can quickly infect the mind of an otherwise rational player and cause you to:

- Swing harder with the driver after making
  a birdie on the previous hole

- Falsely believe that you carry the ball farther
  than you actually do

- Make an unwisely aggressive decision because
  you're "feeling it"

- Expect to play as well as you did the previous round

- Believe you'll never three-putt again after a great practice putting session

- Resist adjusting when part of your game is off

- Assume this chapter doesn't apply to you

Overconfidence is also evident in how you react to missed shots. For example, you might get frustrated when you fail to hit the green with a wedge from the fairway. While your reaction is understandable, the reality is this level of precision simply isn't in everyone's toolkit, at least not yet. You've overestimated the odds of reliably executing that shot. Strokes-gained statistics have helped normalize expectations, but they haven't stopped some players from harboring unrealistic views about their games. Tour pros miss those shots, too; you just don't see those errors very often on TV.

Overconfidence can creep up on any of us. It often does so when you're playing great, shooting low scores, or performing well in practice. A stretch of good holes makes the game feel easy, like you can hit any shot. Then you attempt a shot shape, or a delicate flop, that isn't actually in your arsenal.

A "just go for it" mentality takes hold. You feel as if you can't do anything wrong, so you get lazy with your alignment, care-less with your target, and start playing quicker. You might even recognize that you've gotten a bit sloppy with, say, your ball position or alignment. But you wave it off. "You got this," you tell yourself when, in fact, you don't.

Your euphoria hides the reality that your game is erod-ing beneath your feet. When you're overconfident, you don't realize that your perception, analysis, and execution have already begun to degrade. You're like a cartoon character who has unknowingly run off a cliff and hasn't looked down yet.

You take aggressive lines and swing faster without considering the risk. You lose feel in your short game. Your concentration slips and you become more easily distracted over the ball. You hit riskier shots to preserve momentum. You might even get away with this lapse in process for a while, but once you three-putt from short range, hit a wild tee shot, or suffer a run of bad holes, the shock pierces your veil of invincibility. Now you've looked down, and you're falling.

Overconfidence gives way to anger, frustration, and desperation. You realize the wheels are coming off and double down on bad process to get your game back on track. You tell your playing partner to "watch this," envisioning the perfect shot, and fire right at the pin. But the magic is gone. The golf course doesn't bail out your recklessness. Doubt and confusion swirl as you try to figure out how to get your confidence back.

Ironically, the desire to regain your confidence will land you right back in this spot in the future. Unless you understand and correct the cause of overconfidence, you'll once again have a great round or practice session undone by an inflated view of your game. You don't want that kind of confidence back. Overconfidence is fragile and unstable. You want a quieter kind of confidence. Confidence that's sturdy and consistent.

The Nature of Confidence

Confidence is generally misunderstood. In fact, it may sound strange to suggest that too much confidence is a problem, particularly when entire books have been written claiming that confidence is essential to golf. However, confidence is an emotion, and when any emotion rises too high, the brain malfunctions and performance drops—even when those emotions aren't typically viewed as negative, such as excitement, optimism, or hopefulness.

Confidence is the emotion that reflects how you feel about your skills, knowledge, and experience as a player. Being confident that you'll play well or make a putt doesn't mean you will, just as lacking confidence doesn't mean you won't. How you feel about your game matters less than the reality of your game.

That said, confidence does help you navigate periods when you're working on your game and don't know exactly how to access your capability. It helps you trust your training, execute difficult shots, face uncertainty, learn from mistakes, and adjust to changing conditions. Think of confidence like oil in an engine: too little or too much causes problems. You need the right amount to operate at peak efficiency. Confidence may seem like an innate trait, but it's actually quite fluid and can change instantly.

People—not just golfers—have a natural tendency to believe they're capable, even in the absence of supporting evidence. Research has shown that in Western societies, roughly 60–80 percent of people believe they have above-average intelligence, personality, and attractiveness.[6] In golf, the handicap system has unintentionally turned this tendency into a breeding ground for overconfidence. It creates an illusion where everyone believes they're above average—a statistical impossibility.

Many players get attached to their handicap, falsely believing it represents what they should shoot on a given day. But your handicap doesn't reflect the full bell curve of your performance.

It, too, is widely misunderstood. Your handicap index represents your potential. It's what you're capable of shooting. It's not a prediction of what you'll shoot today. Your index considers your last 20 rounds but omits 12 of your worst. According to the United States Golf Association, players generally shoot their handicap 15–20 percent of the time. In other words, you're expected to play to it about once every five rounds. The other four are not personal failures, despite how they may feel later at dinner.

So yes, it's overconfident to expect to shoot your handicap every time you tee it up. But no, it's not overconfident to want to. Aspiration isn't the problem. Expectation is.

To play your best golf, you need an accurate sense of your ability. In previous chapters, I've discussed faulty views that produce overconfidence. You now understand the perils of believing you've "found it," why you can't expect to always be at your best, how the curated conditions of the driving range can inflate expectations, and how discounting luck leads you to believe you're in more control than you are.

Despite how good you feel, you don't have full control over the outcome of any particular shot. To keep your confidence solid, you must maintain control over your process—your shot selection, routine, and tempo—especially when overconfidence conspires against you.

Keep in mind that you might also believe that by reading this chapter you now "know better" and are immune to future bouts of overconfidence. You aren't. Fixing your mindset isn't that easy, so don't become overconfident about correcting your overconfidence. I told you it was sneaky.

The good news is that you're not blindly overconfident. Your desire to improve is proof of that. It's why you're reading this book.

The Line Between Confidence and Overconfidence

The best time to curb overconfidence is the moment it first arrives. That's usually after a streak of great play. You don't want overconfidence to be the cause of your derailment. To keep the train rolling, you need to recognize it in real time so you can quickly get back on track.

How can you identify overconfidence?

Take a moment and think about the situations where it shows up for you. Does it happen after a massive drive, a long birdie putt, a stretch of great holes, or several good scores in a row? Write those scenarios down.

Then examine how your confidence changes by looking at your thoughts, focus, decisions, actions, physical state, or mistakes. Do you think, "Every drive is going to be this good"? Focus more on making birdies than making good decisions? Grab a club thinking only about the distance to the flag? Play faster or out of turn? Try to ram short putts into the back of the hole?

Write down the signs that are uniquely yours.

Typically, players spot the most obvious signs first. That's a great place to start. As you gain awareness, look for subtler shifts. What's the difference between believing you can pull off a shot and being overconfident? It may not be how you feel, since the sensations are similar. The difference often shows up in shortcuts: rushed decisions, vague targets, or a thought like, "I can make this, no problem."

Here's another way to think about it: Overconfidence isn't just about believing you can hit a shot; it's about how you arrive at that belief. When you're solidly confident, you commit with a clear, specific target. When you're overconfident, you have strong conviction but only a vague direction.

A surge in confidence isn't always a red flag. It can signal real improvement: something clicked and your A-game advanced. Great! Just don't assume it's permanent yet. You still have a C-game that needs reps before it moves forward. Overconfidence convinces you that you own improvements you're still earning. Stay grounded by viewing rising confidence as confirmation of progress, not proof of arrival. Feel good. That's okay. But don't get ahead of yourself.

When you recognize overconfidence, take a step back—figuratively, or literally if you're over the ball—and take a slow breath to remind yourself of what's real.

You've been misled, so remind yourself of the truth: You're fallible, you have a C-game, there are more "its" out there to find, expectations aren't guarantees, and luck still plays a role. You may still choose a risky shot—I'm not trying to be a killjoy; I want you to have fun out there—but at least you'll have accounted for the downside.

Another tactic is something I call "return to B-game." By consciously dialing yourself back—choosing lower-risk shots and avoiding heroics—you preserve momentum and give yourself space to climb back to A-game naturally, with confidence that can actually last.

Sometimes these tactics fail because the real problem isn't overconfidence at all. Instead, it's underconfidence masked as aggression. You attempt miracle shots not because you feel invincible, but because you're hoping a spectacular result will give you confidence you don't currently have. These shots are a form of gambling. Even when they pay off, part of you knows you got lucky. You may ride the high, but you've increased the odds that you'll keep chasing it, and that rarely ends well.

In the next chapter we'll examine the reasons you can get down on your game, and how to find the same solid ground you're looking to find here.

KEY TAKEAWAYS

Overconfidence can inflate your expectations of outcomes you can't fully control. Look out for the line between being confident and believing something about your ability that isn't true.

Your handicap represents your potential, not what you're expected to shoot each round.

Like any emotion, excitement, optimism, or hopefulness can cause the brain to malfunction and performance to drop. Spot the subtle signs—often shortcuts in process—to protect your momentum from being derailed.

CHAPTER 13

Getting Down on Your Game

"I have many moments of glory, but I have
many more moments of very tough times."
— SEVE BALLESTEROS

Golf is hard. Every aspect of the game can get you down and leave you feeling like a car stuck in the mud. Sometimes, with some effort and a little luck, you can get out quickly. Other times, the more you struggle, the deeper you sink, and the more desperate you become.

You can't control where the ball is going, find the center of the clubface, or control your speed on the greens. Your swing becomes tentative, your decisions too conservative. Unsure of what to do, you press, cycling through swing thoughts, trying out new equipment, or hitting the range as soon as the round ends. Nothing works. You abandon process—praying you can knock a long putt close enough for a gimme, hoping you don't hit another big slice, stressing over whether you can escape the bunker.

You feel stuck, unsure how to get your game back, showing up to play hoping for the best but expecting the worst. When the round goes south again, you convince yourself that you don't care and your mind exits stage left. You lose interest, go through the motions, and hit riskier shots. You want the round to be over and wonder why you bother playing this stupid game. Your pace quickens—you're eager to put an end to the agony—convinced that poor play hurts less when you stop trying so hard. It doesn't.

This cycle affects every level of player. Major champions have fallen into the abyss. Ian Baker-Finch lost his game so completely he switched to broadcasting. Tiger's struggles from 2014 to 2017 showed that even the greatest can slip into the darkest of the darkness. If it can happen to them, it can happen to anyone.

Whether it takes a single bad shot to shake your confidence or several poor rounds to wear you down, you may notice some of these clues that you're in a bad spot:

- You talk less and aren't having fun

- You worry about what others think of your game

- You berate yourself with negative thoughts

- You're too deliberate over the ball as your overactive mind grinds away any athleticism

- You feel like you can't do anything right

- You practice without purpose, hoping something will click

- You're more open to unsolicited advice because you don't know what to do

Oddly enough, lacking confidence and having too much of it are caused by the same fundamental problem—believing lies about your game.

One of the more common lies is that one bad swing or round means you'll have more of them. By expecting the worst, your mind predicts a dark future that seems certain. It's not. You're not psychic. You don't know what's going to happen. But you assume today isn't your day and you won't play well. Expecting bad golf shuts your mind off and becomes a self-fulfilling prophecy. You're less focused, more tentative, distrustful of your swing, and uncommitted, and poor process ensures that you don't play well.

Confidence derived from score is fragile. You either have it or you don't. Instead, accounting for various bits of knowledge, experience, and skill forms a base that provides stability.

Think of confidence like a foundation to a house, where all those elements are the building blocks that form it. Regardless of your skill level, you can be confident with the blocks you currently have. When some go missing, your confidence may drop but won't disappear.

You understand that a few bad shots are just a small fraction of your bell curve. Good golf is never far away. You can figure out what's wrong and what adjustments to make. Remember that struggle is an opportunity to improve, you're experienced enough to handle what golf throws at you, and you have stronger elements of your game, like being a good putter or driver of the golf ball. These examples are the blocks your confidence relies on to avoid being overpowered by bad swings or poor rounds.

With enough of them firmly in your mind, you'll have stable confidence.

Stable confidence is the middle ground between overconfidence and lack of confidence, but that doesn't mean you feel neutral or numb. Quite the opposite. You're full of emotion: determined, inspired, courageous, optimistic, peaceful, joyful, and self-assured, to name a few. There's a sense of control and command that comes with it. You'll still have ups and downs, but they're minor and never shift rapidly from one extreme to the other. You focus easily, swing freely, walk tall, trust your sense of what shot to hit, and don't need results to confirm what you already know. You want great results, but don't depend on them like oxygen.

Fixing Cracks in the Foundation

Think of getting down on your game as the mind's way of looking inward to examine what's not working, diagnosing trouble with your technique, decision-making, or mental game. You don't have to feel bad about losing confidence. Clearly something isn't right and all you're doing is trying to figure out what's wrong. In other words, you're problem-solving.

The cause could be as simple as a small kink in your swing, or an inability to play in different course conditions—like high wind, fast greens, or firm fairways—as opposed to a problem in your mental game. When you lose confidence, it can easily be misinterpreted as something mental, when the solution could come from technical improvements or adjustments.

Of course, you might find a faulty perspective affecting you as well. I've already mentioned how negative certainty drives your mind downward. Here are a few other red flags to look out for:

Expecting to Always Be at Your Best

By expecting your A-game, you'll feel worse about struggling or playing poorly—it feels like you have no control. That's an illusion created when playing your best and feeling in total control. One extreme leads to the other. You don't have full control of your A-game; no one does. Ben Hogan famously said that in a good round, he only hit three or four shots exactly as he intended. Playing your best requires full command of all the variables influencing your game, something that's hard for even the best players in the world. Aspire to play your best; don't expect it. Conversely, when your game is off, there are still elements you're in control of. Recognizing the strengths in your game that are still preserved gives you a welcome boost when you see what's missing.

Illusion of Emotional Control

Players who haven't yet worked on their mental game often believe they should always be in control of their emotions, no matter how intense they get. They're unaware that when emotions become overactive, the part of the brain responsible for emotional control stops working properly. If you expect yourself to always be in control of your anger, nerves, or confidence, you'll feel even worse for being steamrolled by intense emotions you weren't prepared to handle. I talked about this in Chapter 6—emotions are powerful. Prepare to counter them, but don't expect to.

Premature Sense of Mastery

When playing well, you can easily be fooled into thinking that you've mastered aspects of your game that you're still training. You feel in such command that you convince yourself you've achieved Unconscious Competence and will never slip from that position. The truth of your still-evolving skills is a painful reveal. Confidence plummets after taking steps backward in competition, playing a more challenging course, or coping with rust after an extended break. It feels like you're back to square one, a classic overreaction. Mastery takes longer to achieve than most players realize. Before understanding the learning process, you didn't realize that those skills were still being acquired and required more reps. You got ahead of yourself because you didn't have the theory or structure to be realistic.

Whenever you lose confidence, examine your mind for the lies it believes and anchor yourself to what's real. The right perspective gives you solid, unshakable confidence regardless of how good you are at golf. That is, unless your confidence has been damaged by high expectations or standards of perfectionism. This unique scenario—where high standards subtly erode confidence from within—doesn't cause an obvious loss of confidence; instead it quietly undermines it.

Correct the Damage from Perfectionism and High Expectations

Many of you are high achievers, driven to excel at whatever you put your mind to. Those high expectations propel you to success in other endeavors, but in golf they can produce downsides you don't fully realize. While you know golf is a game that can't be perfected, you still expect too much of yourself, and that undercuts your progress.

In a game so fraught with imperfection, so many of you struggle to accept off days, and can't help but:

- Place a lot of pressure on yourself to be great

- Second-guess many of your decisions

- Get frustrated by bad outcomes beyond your control

- Be superstitious with your preparation

- Obsess over all aspects of a shot

- Fail to applaud good results

- Become self-critical over slight missteps

- Carry regret from one round to the next, having
  a hard time getting over mistakes or poor play

- Always think you could have shot lower, even after
  a great round

- Care more about how your swing looks than how
  it performs

I want all of you to realize your golfing dreams, but that won't happen if your expectations loom so large they damage confidence. Perfectionism and high expectations can be a double-edged sword where one side drives your motivation to work incredibly hard to realize your outsized goals, while the other side cuts you down. It's an interesting dichotomy. On one hand, to have these high expectations you must believe deeply in yourself. Yet when things go wrong, you overreact and berate yourself.

Instead, let's transform perfectionism into something more productive by blunting one edge of the sword to stop the self-inflicted damage, while sharpening the other side that drives you to excel.

The Inchworm Concept is the antidote. It's not about being perfect. No one is. We all have a C-game. We all have relative weaknesses, always. But that doesn't mean we can't, at times, reach our own version of perfection by maximizing our capabilities in that moment.

Inchworm shows us that perfection is a moving target you've already achieved many times before, as measured by your bell curve then. You've hit perfect shots and played the perfect round. And once you reach the peak in your capability, a new definition of perfection emerges, the standard rises, giving way to the potential for the front end of your Inchworm to move forward. That's where you stand now. What will allow you to climb to greater heights? To become more perfect, you must embrace imperfection.

Your version of perfectionism isn't practical. It shuns and demonizes imperfection rather than leveraging it for insights that yield growth. Appreciate the benchmark you've established and what it took to get there. Balance your hard-driving mind with a perspective that recognizes great play and values improvement. Determine how to move your B- and C-game forward when you inevitably fall short, as those parts of your game provide the easiest path to reach perfection once again. Or, change your focus from seeking perfection in outcome to striving for it in your process—control the controllables.

Shifting your perspective on perfection is a critical first step. You also need to heal the damage to your confidence created by your high expectations or perfectionistic standards. Here's how.

All of us have an internal measuring stick to gauge how we're performing. If this were a game, you'd gain or lose points based on the quality of every shot you hit or round you play. Expectations set the baseline and reaching that level earns you zero points—you don't get credit for doing what you're supposed to do. Only when you exceed expectations do you earn points, which is incredibly hard given the standard is set so high. Most of the time you lose points. In this game, points equal confidence. So where does that leave you? In a hole. Exactly how you feel at times.

High expectations initially dig this hole, but as this problem evolves, there's a subtle sense that reaching perfection is how to get out. If you could perform perfectly, you'd instantly escape and would consistently and justifiably feel confident again.

This is a myth. Once you reach a new height in performance, you'll once again expect an even lower score, better handicap, or bigger victory. Satisfaction is fleeting. The goal-posts move again and the hole gets deeper. External sources—even heaps of praise from others—can't fill it. Only you can, by recalibrating your internal measuring stick with goals, not expectations.

The two words may seem interchangeable, but the difference between expectations and goals is significant.

An expectation is an implied guarantee that you'll attain the outcome you want, which means always having the requisite skill accessible. Expectations demand outcomes without concern about how you get there. Thus, faced with setbacks, mistakes, or failures along the way, expectations leave you unprepared and self-critical.

Goals imply unknowns, learning, and ups and downs as you navigate an undefined road. They assume the potential for challenge and hardship, and welcome the lessons that setbacks, mistakes, and failure provide. You assess how or why you failed, where progress emerged, and how you'll do better next time. Goals provide many points to derive pride and satisfaction—not just at the finish line. The net result is a stronger foundation of confidence that you leverage to pursue what's next.

To be clear, I'm not asking you to lower your expectations. No. I want your aspirations to be as high as you want. The problem is not that you want to be perfect; it's that you expect it. The correction is not to lower your expectations. Instead, convert them into goals so you stop digging a deeper hole.

The last step: fill the hole. Go back into your golfing history and correct the previous damage from your old standard.

Obviously, you can't change what has happened in the past, but you can recover the lost confidence that you earned but didn't realize. Very often there are past accomplishments or benchmarks that weren't given proper respect or acknowledgment. It doesn't matter if your friends, playing partners, or club members lauded you with praise—your perspective is what matters.

Go back and look at all the accomplishments you've had since the start of your golf career—the first time you broke 70, 80, or 100, winning a club event, reaching a new standard of ball-striking, becoming a good putter. Big or small, write down as many of your accomplishments as you can, especially the ones where you didn't feel particularly proud, but deserved to.

Keep an eye out for the "Yeah, buts" as you complete this task. This common phrase is used to downplay what you've attained.

"Yeah, but I could have saved a few shots."

"Yeah, but it's only the third flight."

"Yeah, but I'm still a 20-handicap."

"Yeah, but it's not the U.S. Open."

Own what you've attained. More is always out there; it's how golf works. It also happens to be the way of the world.

Then examine each accomplishment by noting how you did it. What were the steps? What did you learn? What difficulties did you encounter and how did you conquer them? How was it a building block to where your game is today?

Do this regularly for 5 to 15 minutes. It's not a task you do once and never again. Think of it this way: You've been starved of the confidence you deserve—one big meal won't satisfy you, only regular consumption will.

Once you've gone through this process for all your accomplishments, review them. You might learn more as you go through a second round, further instill the correction, and strengthen this new way of evaluating yourself.

Taken together, your intense drive to be great, even perfect, will have the stable confidence needed to drive your game to new heights. It might also remove embarrassment. But if not, the next chapter addresses this common problem not always associated with a weakness in confidence.

KEY TAKEAWAYS

Don't feel bad about losing confidence. This is your mind's way of looking inward to solve what's not working in your game.

Every player, regardless of ability, can build stable confidence by correcting faulty perspectives and valuing their knowledge, experience, and skill.

Perfectionism and high expectations drive motivation but also damage confidence. Transform them by converting expectations into goals.

Perfection is a moving target. To become more perfect, you must embrace imperfection.

CHAPTER 14

Fear of Embarrassment

"Golf's something that I do. It's a tremendously huge part
of my life. But it doesn't define me as a person."
— SCOTTIE SCHEFFLER

Golf can make us look silly. If you're uncomfortable with that possibility, you might naturally fear embarrassing yourself when playing through a group, lining up a short putt to win the match, or chipping from a tight lie where you might blade it over the green.

You may fear embarrassing yourself even before teeing it up, like playing in a scramble with work colleagues or when you're in a slump struggling to make consistent contact. These situations make you more self-conscious, suspicious of what others think about you, and sensitive to comments—which, unfortunately, only ratchets up the tension or nerves, and in turn, increases the likelihood of the terrible outcomes you fear. Sigh.

Intellectually, you know there's nothing to worry about. Other golfers are far more concerned with their own game than with yours. Plus, if you're playing poorly but not holding up play, they'll sympathize or crack some jokes to lighten the mood. We've all been there.

The reality is, the fear of embarrassment has nothing to do with what other players think about your shots, score, or handicap and instead centers on what you think. You might fear negative comments and harsh critiques from other players, but they're figments of your imagination. While you suspect your playing partner is thinking something like "how could you miss such an easy putt," they're probably not. And even if they were, why would missing an easy putt be embarrassing? The miss doesn't cause embarrassment—everyone misses, including the best in the world. It's how you view it.

Think about it: You're not affected by comments you know are incorrect. If your playing partner said you were playing like a purple dinosaur from the planet Blee Bop, you wouldn't be embarrassed by such an absurd accusation. You'd question their sanity, not your golf game. You don't just fear comments from other players. You fear not living up to your own expectations and the self-criticism that follows. But you also care what they think. The key is recognizing that their opinion matters far less than yours, and that you're the one who has to live with your reaction.

Embarrassment feeds on the dissatisfaction of preexisting weaknesses, much like how you wince, flinch, or dodge someone touching a bruise on your shoulder. Here, the bruise is your distaste for your handicap going up, duffing an easy chip, snap-hooking a drive in front of a crowd, or the hitch in your swing. But if you don't feel bad about your weak points, there's no bruise and nothing for you to be embarrassed by. You just play golf.

Embarrassing situations will happen again and a fresh outlook can change how you respond. Accept the reality of your game, acknowledge your weaknesses, realize you're strong enough to handle them, and don't shy away from the moment. Your opinion is more important than what others think. Be proud of handling yourself with the kind of character you want to demonstrate. Any comments actually voiced by someone else speak more to their character than yours.

Once you start to change the nature of how you handle these situations, the less you'll need to protect against future embarrassment. Then, when you feel the tension and doubt ratcheting up, remind yourself that there is nothing to fear anymore. The worst-case scenario isn't that bad. Sure, you'd love to hit a great shot or sink a winning putt, but if that doesn't happen, you won't feel the scarring pain of embarrassment.

Play out the worst-case scenario in your mind. You blade the chip over the green. Maybe you make double bogey. Someone might chuckle. Then…what? Everyone moves to the next hole and forgets about it in 30 seconds. How bad is that really? When you realize the worst case isn't actually catastrophic, the fear loses its power.

If your progress stalls, especially in challenging situations, it's possible there's more on the line than just embarrassment. The game may have become too personal.

When Golf Gets Personal

Is your identity so wrapped up in golf that how you feel about yourself is on the line every time you play? Golf obviously is important to you, but problems arise when golf comes to define you.

Consider these questions to gauge if the game has become too personal:

- Do you put a lot of pressure on yourself to play well?

- Is your mood, focus, or emotional state off the course heavily influenced by what happens on the course?

- When playing poorly, or in a slump, do you feel lost or hopeless?

- Do you have thoughts like "I'm a failure," "I'm a loser," or "how I played was shameful"?

- Is golf such a big obsession that it negatively affects other aspects of your life?

- Do you avoid taking time off even when you know you should?

- Is it hard to describe yourself in a way that isn't related to golf?

- If you couldn't play golf for a couple years, would you feel bad about yourself or struggle to even know what to do with your time?

The more you answered "yes" to these questions, the more likely personal confidence, identity, or self-worth hinges on your performance in golf. When golf plays too large a role in how you feel about yourself, or how you establish your personal confidence, it's hard for your mentality to be stable. This might explain why you're so fixated on technique, scoring, handicap, or winning. Your sense of self depends on it.

As severe as this problem may seem—and the highs and lows can be pretty intense—the answer can be quite simple. You've lost sight of the independent parts of yourself that transcend golf. This can be especially true for those of you who started playing golf at an early age, since kids are most prone to defining themselves by their competence in the game. Golf, like other things we do in life, has a way of teaching us about ourselves. We're not born knowing our talents, personalities, values, beliefs, or goals. We interact with the world and in doing so come to define ourselves.

Playing bad golf makes you feel like you're losing a part of yourself, but that's an illusion. Success or failure on the course doesn't materially change your identity. There are elements that are always preserved and, ideally, enhanced, regardless of the outcome. You gain resilience. You find new areas of strength and a higher level of skill when excelling.

To make golf feel less like a measure of your identity, take some time to define and embrace your core characteristics, values, beliefs, and goals that are independent from golf performance and would still be true even if you couldn't play another round.

I suggest brainstorming for 5 to 10 minutes per day to uncover details that may not immediately come to mind. Be comprehensive. For instance, characteristics could be "hard-working, intelligent, resourceful." Values might include things like "being honest, trustworthy, and a reliable friend." Beliefs might be "you get out what you put in," "life isn't always fair but that won't stop me from being successful," and "how you carry yourself on the course is more important than how you play." Goals might be "have fun," "have the freedom to pursue my biggest ambitions," or "be a good friend, parent, or member of the community."

The key to this exercise is that you're not aspiring toward a better version of yourself. You're recognizing existing aspects that remain true no matter the state of your game or how you're playing. A bad shot, bad round, or even a bad season can never take them away.

Once you have the details down, regularly review and test yourself until you reach the point where you're not living and dying on each shot or round. The stronger your connection, the harder it is to be shaken, and each experience becomes additive. After about four to six weeks, you should feel more solid about yourself and feel less of a need to play great golf. Mind you, this doesn't mean you will be any less competitive or hungry to play great golf and achieve your golfing goals. It means you get to tee it up without feeling like your life depends on it. Isn't that nice?

Instability in confidence is a big contributor to the inability to handle pressure. But it's not the only cause. If nerves tend to get the best of you, whether on the first tee, the last green, or anywhere in between, check out the next chapter for more on how to thrive when feeling the heat.

KEY TAKEAWAYS

Embarrassment isn't about what others think; it's your distaste for weakness in your game that causes so much anguish.

Golf obviously is important, but never lose sight of the independent parts of yourself that transcend the game.

CHAPTER 15

When Nerves Get the Best of You

"A lot of guys who have never choked
have never been in the position to do so."

— TOM WATSON

In pressure situations, it's normal to feel anxious, nervous, excited, amped, or all of the above. Ideally, nerves fuel your best golf, as they do for most top professionals, elite amateurs, and even some everyday golfers. That surge of energy and emotion primes your senses, deepening your focus, sharpening your thinking, and opening your eyes to details you might otherwise miss, like a subtle undulation in the green.

At the right level of intensity, pressure can ignite peak performance and increase your chances of getting into the zone. Pressure, however, has a tipping point. Cross it, and those same nerves begin working against you. Whether in competition or a casual round, nerves can overtake you at any moment. Worry, doubt, and fear quicken your tempo, send your thoughts swirling, make your hands numb, and create tension throughout your body.

Here are a few common scenarios where this happens:

- On the first tee, you feel the added strain to play well and get off to a good start

- Facing a shot over water with out-of-bounds on the right, you focus more on what can go wrong than on committing to the right shot

- Playing a great round, your mind jumps ahead to calculate what you need to post your lowest score ever

- Over short putts you're expected to make, your hands get jittery, you second-guess your read, and make a weak, uncommitted stroke, hoping it somehow falls

- Playing in front of a crowd, you go through your routine, but mostly to look like you know what you're doing

- Feeling pushed by the group behind you, you swing faster and play faster, even if they can't play through

- Down the stretch in contention to win, your stomach tightens, your mind goes blank, and you struggle to get comfortable over the ball

- Paired with better players, you become self-conscious, cycle through swing thoughts, and can't get your swing to feel right

When Tour pros are in contention, you often hear them say they welcome the pressure. It means they're in the mix and playing golf that matters. Something similar applies to golfers of all stripes. Feeling pressure means you care. You want to play well, hit quality shots, beat your buddies, win a club event. Success in golf is important to you. You also want to have fun, but the energy and effort you put into the game naturally raise the stakes. When the stakes rise, pressure follows.

For those who tend to shake more than they can shake off their nerves, here are some ideas to help you use pressure to play well when it matters most.

Start with a change in perspective. Pressure itself isn't bad. Excess pressure is what causes problems. A common reason pressure becomes excessive is believing the physical changes in your body are a problem and the reason you perform poorly.

You're uncomfortable. You can't swallow. Your palms are sweaty. Your heart races. Your mind goes into overdrive. Your grip tightens. Nothing feels right. You assume this is a problem, and that belief pushes you to try to get rid of the nervousness and return to how golf is "supposed" to feel. Deep breathing helps a bit. Focusing on your pre-shot routine offers temporary relief.

But the physical sensations that come with nerves are completely normal. Trying to escape what feels like a problem keeps you from embracing the challenge, acclimating to the experience, and learning how to perform well under fire.

You may have played far below your expectations in pressure-packed moments before, but pressure itself likely wasn't the cause. Even if you're visibly shaking or can't feel your hands, your muscles remain primed to perform, not fail.

A powerful example came at the 2022 Open Championship at St Andrews. Cameron Smith pulled into a tie for the lead late in the final round. When he noticed where he stood, he admitted later, his hands went numb and stayed that way the rest of the day. Nothing about his internal state suggested comfort or control. Yet Smith continued to play steady, disciplined golf and was spectacular on the greens. Nowhere was that more evident than at the 17th hole, where he putted from off the green, curling the ball around the notorious Road Hole bunker to save par under suffocating pressure. The nerves didn't disappear. The sensations didn't improve. But they also didn't stand in the way of brilliance.

Pressure itself isn't the problem. What it does to your attention is.

Because you don't often experience pressure this intense on the golf course, its novelty pulls your focus inward. You become preoccupied with how your body feels rather than what the shot requires. At its core, pressure distracts.

Not convinced? I suggest an experiment. On a day when you're playing a relaxed round, try hitting a shot while focusing primarily on the sensation in your feet. Pay close attention to how your feet feel as you select a club, walk onto the tee, take a practice swing, set up, and hit the shot. You'll almost certainly hit it worse. The swing didn't change; your process did. With less focus on the shot itself, weaknesses surface and you lose the information needed to be athletic. Pressure works the same way when it consumes too much of your attention.

This is one reason many players rely on a consistent pre-shot routine. It helps direct focus outward, toward the task at hand. But don't force the appearance of a consistent pre-shot routine; it must function properly to help you play well under pressure.

Remind yourself that feeling pressure won't cause a poor shot unless it distracts you. Push back against the inward pull by feeding your mind and swing the information they need. This is challenging, and repetition makes it easier.

You'll find more chances to practice when you stop taking mulligans and conceding short putts. If handling pressure better matters to you, every opportunity counts. You can't recreate real consequence on the range or during casual rounds. Mulligans and gimmies protect the scorecard and confidence, but they remove consequence from the game and limit your ability to strengthen your process under pressure.

Oddly enough, another valuable opportunity appears when you're playing poorly.

When things go wrong, frustration and despair creep in quickly, and staying present becomes difficult. Focus slips, tension builds, shot-making suffers, and you want the round to end. The experience closely resembles what happens when you feel pressure with a chance to go low.

When you're playing really well, anxiety and excitement create a similar challenge. Though these situations sit on opposite ends of the emotional spectrum, they demand the same skill: staying focused, committed, and disciplined.

The next time nothing goes your way, fight to make better decisions. Stay committed. Choose smart targets. Make thoughtful adjustments. A stronger process during bad rounds prepares you to handle pressure when it matters most.

Whether your score is good or bad, resist the temptation to give in or give up. Maintain your process. This isn't easy, and that difficulty gives it value. Growth doesn't come from comfort. Pressure is the weight you don't get on the range.

Build consistency in your process and, over time, you'll handle pressure better. Still, some players need a more potent antidote to quiet the extra nerves, anxiety, and tension that pressure-packed moments create.

Certainty Is the Antidote to Fear

Golf can generate enough anxiety and fear to neutralize everything you've just read. When that happens, relief can come from a surprising place: certainty.

When anxiety takes over, the mind races. It searches for answers, second-guesses decisions, and tries desperately to avoid embarrassment, costly mistakes, or a spectacular collapse.

Certainty calms that chaos. When you know what's going to happen, pressure fades. Certainty and fear can't coexist.

Imagine a magical golfing wizard appearing before you tee off in a tournament and telling you exactly how you'll play and what you'll shoot. The tension would disappear immediately. You might not like what you hear, but you wouldn't feel anxious. You'd already know.

Certainty is among the most effective ways to reduce intense pressure. This helps explain why overconfident players often seem immune to it. Their conviction blocks uncertainty. This isn't a suggestion to adopt bravado or pretend you have the game figured out. It simply illustrates the principle. Trying to force confidence relies on the mind, which pressure can easily overwhelm. Genuine certainty holds up better.

But how do you create certainty in a game defined by uncertainty?

First, avoid negative certainty. Under pressure, the mind searches for certainty but often lands in the wrong place, like becoming convinced you're about to miss an important putt.

Second, build a list of things you can be certain of during a shot or round. Players who thrive under pressure have reduced unknowns in their game, both big and small. Building stable confidence, as discussed in Chapter 13, plays a major role. You develop certainty about your skills, your experience, and what you've already accomplished.

Consider the following examples of things you can be certain of and build your own list:

- You've hit shots like this well in the past
- You've made a clear decision, and you won't
  know if it was right until after the shot

- Strong parts of your swing, such as balance, rhythm, or tempo, hold up under pressure

- You're a good putter, and missed putts are part of the game

- Your identity isn't on the line

- You'd rather risk embarrassment than hit a weak, uncommitted shot

- Failure teaches you more than spectators ever will

- You don't control outcomes completely

- What you're feeling is normal and common

- You've already accomplished meaningful things in golf

- You enjoy a good challenge, and pressure doesn't arise for easy tasks

- Your friends will razz you for missing, and that's part of the fun

With experience, you'll also gain certainty about how pressure affects your swing. You'll learn which muscles tighten, how far the ball flies, and how to maintain feel on and around the greens even when your hands feel numb or shaky.

Create your own list and review it before rounds likely to spark pressure. You can't remove uncertainty from the game, but each layer of certainty fills a gap and reduces excess nervousness enough to help you perform.

Anger can also ignite nerves. Playing below your capability often unleashes self-criticism and the fear of losing. Those emotions only add fuel to the flames. Let's put them out in the next chapter.

KEY TAKEAWAYS

Pressure is normal, not bad. It means you care. Embrace the experience and don't let it distract your process.

Take fewer mulligans and gimmies to practice handling pressure.

Certainty is the antidote to fear, anxiety, and excessive nerves. Think about the things you can be certain of in your game and use that to settle your mind.

CHAPTER 16

The Frustration of Playing Poorly

"Golf is the only sport where you
shout at yourself and
nobody else can hear you."

— LEE TREVINO

Some days are a struggle. You're playing lousy, losing balls, making brain-dead doubles, and can't get anything going. You finally hit a good drive only to chunk your approach shot. Around the green you give more shots away, stubbing easy chips and failing to get up and down. The game is unforgiving and full of landmines. It's maddening.

And then it gets worse.

Frustration boils over and causes you to make mistakes that are so blatantly obvious you know immediately what you did wrong. Or worse, you know beforehand. A little voice in your head tells you that you're aimed too far left, don't have enough club, or didn't account for the wind. And yet you don't back off. It doesn't make sense why you can't stop doing something you know is wrong. You know better! That realization is like pouring gas on the fire.

Your anger sparks demeaning and berating thoughts. "How could you be so stupid!?" "What the heck are you doing!?" "You're a joke!" Expletives fly out of your mouth and, quite possibly, the club from your hands.

You don't want to feel this angry and know you shouldn't—it's just a game, after all—but treating it as such is easier said than done.

Here's what you need to understand: Being frustrated by poor play is reasonable. You want to play well and aren't performing up to the standard you expect from yourself. You wish you could achieve the kind of monastic calm that makes a bad shot feel like a learning opportunity. But you can't. Mediocre play bothers you. That's okay. Anger isn't inherently a bad thing, so long as you let it out in a way that doesn't damage the course or your reputation, and, just as important, allows you to move on to the next shot unfazed by the prior one.

The problem isn't the anger itself; it's what happens when it overtakes you.

You can't let go of past miscues, so you swing harder, take risks trying to make up for bad shots, and compound one bad decision with another. Or you give up, trying to make it look like you don't care, all while the terrible play eats at you inside.

It may be hard to understand how you could do something you know is wrong, but here's the answer: Obvious mistakes are inevitable when frustration becomes too intense. The real mistake isn't swinging too hard or not backing off. It's failing to notice the increase in frustration and taking action to avoid reaching this point.

Understanding why requires looking at the relationship between your mental state and performance level.

When playing great, your mental game is in an optimal state. You're in the zone, or close to it, full of energy, and emotionally stable, so you execute at a high level and make quality decisions. Any mistakes at this level you couldn't know about beforehand. Frankly, to even call them "mistakes" is a stretch. You wouldn't say a toddler learning to walk is making a mistake when they fall. Your attempts to take your A-game higher are no different. These "learning mistakes" can't be prevented. This is what happens when you run into the upper range of your ability.

C–GAME	B–GAME	A–GAME
OBVIOUS MISTAKES	**MARGINAL MISTAKES**	**LEARNING MISTAKES**
CAUSE: Your emotions are too intense or your energy is too low. (Physical limitation or injury.)	CAUSE: A blend of weakness in your technique, decision-making, physicality, and/ or mental game.	CAUSE: Unknowable weakness in your technique, decision-making, and/or physicality.

On the flip side, your C-game is caused by intense emotions or a lack of energy and focus, not a gap in knowledge or skill. You know what to do, but excess emotion or lagging energy prevents you from accessing it. That's why you're so quick to recognize when you do something wrong yet powerless to stop it.

To complete the picture, B-game is a blend of mental and technical strengths and weaknesses. You make some marginal tactical errors—things that need improvement but aren't glaringly obvious—while making plenty of good decisions.

Mentally and emotionally, you'll have impulses or thoughts like you do in your C-game, but still have the presence of mind, mental energy, focus, and emotional control to avoid succumbing to them.

You're not always going to play your best, and when you don't, your first priority is to avoid compounding the mistakes that make bad rounds even worse. This is another version of sucking less. The first correction to make: stop beating yourself up.

Self-Criticism Makes You Play Worse

Self-criticism is a habit many of you fall into when things start to go awry. Sure, it can be motivational when your mistakes are caused by apathy, distraction, or fatigue, providing the necessary kick in the backside to get your head in the game.

But this becomes a self-perpetuating problem. You inadvertently train yourself to rely on self-criticism to motivate you to play your best. Without it, your motivation dips and your game slips backward. After a streak of great play, for instance, you get complacent, lose focus, lack intensity. This inevitably leads to mistakes, you beat yourself up, your motivation returns, and the cycle eventually repeats. Self-criticism is a great motivator, but mistakes and poor play are the price you pay for it.

When poor play is caused by low confidence, frustration, overconfidence, or anxiety, self-criticism intensifies your emotions so much that you can't avoid obvious mistakes. Plus, it creates another cycle that's hard to escape.

Self-criticism tends to be more punishing than clarifying. You berate yourself more for what went wrong than you examine why it went wrong. This keeps the real problem bur-ied and unresolved, meaning you'll be right back in this position when those emotions resurface.

To stop self-criticism from causing your own demise, con-vert your critiques into curiosity. Taking a moment to shift your perspective during the round can help break the fever and free you to find a practical adjustment.

Start by gauging whether your emotions were too high or your energy was too low. This is important because players often fail to notice subtle drops in energy, and frustration or self-criticism might be the first indication. For example, maybe a change in energy or emotion doesn't immediately lead to a miscue, and the first one doesn't even get you mad, but eventu-ally, after a few more poorly executed shots or missed putts, you notice frustration building.

Make a quick note in your phone or on the scorecard about what changed in your emotions, energy, or mentality. Writing down these observations is especially important to make it obvious what went wrong and spot trends. Sometimes it's easy to get stuck in your head. Writing helps clarify what you're deal-ing with and that alone can put your mind at ease. You might notice numerous signs that frustration was building: walking at a quicker pace, added grip pressure, overswinging, careless decisions, carrying regret to the next hole. Be curious about what you find, not critical of it.

Spotting these signals or knowing what caused the initial drop in performance may not immediately get you back to playing well (although it can), or prevent it from happen-ing again, but it can help your mind escape the criticism and refocus on the right thing to fix. If that helps you avoid the raging bonfire that blows your round up, you've taken a firm step forward and can tackle the initial reason for underperforming.

Often, that initial reason traces back to what you expected from yourself. Throughout the book I've examined ways your mental game contributes to substandard play—overconfidence, fear, heated reactions to bad luck. Soon I'll talk about others, like distractions and slow play. But first, let's look at two common sources of frustration: unrealistic expectations and an inability to handle losing.

Unrealistic Expectations

Golf doesn't always provide perfect feedback, so it can be difficult to know what's reasonable to expect from your game. Frustration makes it easy to find out—it's the output of your unrealistic expectations colliding with reality.

In those instances where you feel frustrated or angry, ask yourself "what was I expecting?" This gives you a quick way of uncovering the real source of what can tilt your mental game out of alignment.

Players harbor countless expectations, but here are the most common:

- Hitting every green with a wedge
- Never three-putting
- Playing perfectly every round
- Never losing command with the driver
- Always gauging the wind correctly

- Never getting a bad break

- Hitting the ball on the course like you do in practice

- Never missing three-footers

- Always controlling your emotions

Naturally you get frustrated, even angry, whenever you miss a green, three-putt, underperform, or spray the driver. But as I outlined in Chapter 13, expectations are guarantees. Being assured of uncertain outcomes is overconfident. You're believing a lie and frustration helps you discover it.

Here's the reality: Only your C-game is guaranteed. Your worst is the only thing that's always accessible, regardless of how tired, angry, overconfident, or distracted you are. Everything else—your A-game and B-game—is earned through your preparation, rest, being in reasonable physical shape, understanding adjustments to your swing, and applying corrections to your mental game. I'm not suggesting that your worst is what will happen. But, practically speaking, the biggest value that expectations provide is defining the "floor" of your game.

Expectations need to be the floor, not the ceiling. There's integrity and strength to a floor, and knowing yours helps provide stability for your mentality. The ceiling is the aspiration you're reaching toward. But when you expect yourself to perform at that high level every time you tee it up, you're setting yourself up for frustration and an erosion of confidence. That's why it's important you understand your true expectations, convert reasonable ones into goals, and eliminate the unreasonable ones, such as expecting to always play your best. As your

C-game improves, your floor rises, inch by inch, eventually making it easier to reach the standard you previously expected. Strive for more, but don't expect it.

To help you better determine reasonable expectations, you may also find value in statistics. Some of you are unknowingly expecting yourself to perform at levels reserved for professionals. For example, do you expect yourself to make every three-footer? It's time to recalibrate.

As Mark Broadie, the inventor of the "Strokes Gained" statistic, highlighted in his book *Every Shot Counts*, PGA Tour players miss 4% of putts from that length and players who shoot in the 90s miss 16%. On putts from five feet, PGA Tour players only make 77%, a scratch golfer makes 66%, and a player who shoots in the 90s makes 50%. By all means, try your best to make every one of those putts. But when you don't (and you won't!), you can avoid lingering frustration by understanding it'll happen once out of every two or three attempts on average.

Stats aren't for everyone, but some basics can help normalize the frequency of outcomes and help you adjust expectations. I suggest checking out Jon Sherman's book *The Four Foundations of Golf.* He does a great job of making stats accessible.

Hating to Lose

Being fiercely competitive is a trait shared by many great golfers. Like them, you enjoy putting your game to the test in a tournament, club event, or regular game with your group. Your competitive drive can blaze as hot as you want, as long as it doesn't burn you.

Problems arise when your drive to win is paired with an inability to handle rounds where you're struggling and can't get any momentum going. No one wants to lose, and while many of you are okay losing when you play well, some of you hate losing so much that you'll make choices that are out of character—losing control, storming off the course, even cheating.

Great competitors don't lose control because they're strong enough to handle the pain of losing. They're like boxers with an iron chin who can take a punch. If the pain of losing is so great that instinctively you'll do anything to avoid it, you may be suffering from a phenomenon called Prospect Theory.[7] Renowned psychologists Daniel Kahneman and Amos Tversky (you may know Kahneman from his popular book *Thinking, Fast and Slow*) found that for many people losing money hurts more than winning money feels good. Consequently, people are more likely to take greater risk to avoid losing money and become risk-averse to preserve gains. A similar phenomenon occurs in golf and may explain why you play more conservatively when you have a great round going.

In other words, golf can give you more reasons to feel bad about losing than to feel good about winning. This renders winning more of an escape from the torture of losing than something that generates considerable positive emotion. That's why you hate losing so much. It hurts, and much more than winning feels good.

The good news is that Prospect Theory is an observation, not a law of human nature. It's not like gravity. You can overcome it. Kahneman and Tversky agree that a change in perspective can recalibrate the value of winning and losing and curb this dynamic.[8]

So there's no confusion, I'm not trying to convince you to enjoy losing. I want you to have a better chance of winning! Here are a few ideas how:

Elevate Winning

Winning isn't an accident when you bring the right intensity, make quality decisions, execute at a high level, face challenging shots, and battle through pressure moments. Elevate the significance of winning by emphasizing what it took. You earned it through time spent refining your technique, learning various shots, developing feel around the greens, honing shot selection. Winning and playing well confirms what you've put into the game. You deserve to feel pride and satisfaction for that. I'm not suggesting you throw a giant celebration. Simply take a moment after the round to acknowledge what it took to get here. Valuing winning this way will also protect you from the overconfidence that comes from expecting to win or play well again next round. Sometimes players purposely restrict themselves from feeling the joy of winning to avoid falling into this trap. But you can avoid it by viewing winning as confirmation of the past, not a prediction of the future.

Acclimate to Pain

Don't assume that pain is negative. For people who are highly competitive, losing will never feel good and that's okay. It's simply a result of your competitiveness and intense desire to win. Some of you may have a low tolerance for losing because you haven't experienced much of it outside of golf. You've been pretty good at everything you put your mind to, successful in school, your career, and elsewhere. Sometimes pain is just pain, and you have to get used to it. Embracing it makes the experience more tolerable. You'll learn that the pain from losing will dissipate, usually a lot faster than you anticipate. You get used to the feeling and build up the strength to handle it. Jack Nicklaus, who finished second in a record 19 majors—more than the record 18 he won—was famous for his grace in defeat. He understood that losing more than you win is part of being a great competitor. You build resilience by experiencing loss and learning you can handle it. Here's a practical way to become tougher: Feel the pain and then talk through it as a great coach would. Dig in and push yourself to stay the course, select the right shot, don't beat yourself up, stick with what you know works. The pain is always worse when you make mistakes trying to avoid it during the round, and it sticks around longer when you run from it afterwards.

Frustration on the golf course is all too common, but it doesn't have to derail your round. Whether it's converting self-criticism into curiosity, recalibrating unrealistic expectations, or learning to handle the pain of losing, these adjustments help you stay in control when things go sideways.

Sometimes fighting fire with fire is how to lower the temperature. In your head, say the word "No" or "Stop" with convincing force. This is how you give your Injecting Logic statement a chance to change your perspective quickly and get you back on solid emotional ground.

The goal isn't to eliminate frustration; that's unrealistic. The goal is to recognize it early and respond in ways that keep you playing your game instead of undermining it.

As I mentioned, lapses in focus often contribute to the initial mistakes that can spark frustration and self-criticism. Don't get distracted. I'll tackle that next.

KEY TAKEAWAYS

Obvious mistakes are inevitable when frustration becomes too intense. You must notice the rise in frustration early—and take action then—to avoid costing yourself more shots.

Be curious, not critical. There's always a reason for underperforming; only by understanding why can you make meaningful improvements.

Expectations are ideally the floor that supports your game, not unreasonable standards causing overreactions. Convert reasonable ones into goals and recognize progress along the way.

Losing doesn't have to hurt more than winning feels good. Elevate winning and acclimate to the pain.

CHAPTER 17

Distracted Driving

*"What do I mean by concentration? I mean focusing
totally on the business at hand and commanding
your body to do exactly what you want it to do."*

— ARNOLD PALMER

We live in a distracted world, and golfers are not immune. Just as driving a car while distracted by your phone is hazardous to your health, driving a golf ball while distracted is hazardous to your game.

Distraction in everyday life has become so normalized that many players don't realize how much it affects their focus on the course. We're accustomed to splitting our attention: checking phones, multitasking, filling every quiet moment with stimulation. Golf is often meant to be an escape from this onslaught, a chance to clear your head, step away from screens, and enjoy being outside. But a mind trained to seek constant novelty doesn't always settle just because you tee it up.

On the course, lapses in focus rarely announce themselves. Sometimes there's an obvious interruption—movement in your backswing, a cart screeching at the wrong time, a ball landing near the green while you're putting, an unoriginal comedian screaming "fore" from a passing car—but these are relatively rare and often unavoidable. More common, and more costly, are the quiet moments when your attention drifts and you give away a few shots without fully realizing why.

You step onto the tee still thinking about a three-putt on the previous hole and forget to rehearse the move you're working on. Slow pace of play prolongs the round, momentum fades, and stray thoughts creep in as you're over the ball. Midway through a frustrating round, you sink into negative self-talk, or scroll through emails, searching for a better use of your energy.

These small lapses don't always cost you immediately. You've played enough golf to hit quality shots and make putts on autopilot. Eventually, though, you face a shot that demands clear intent and adjustment, and if your mind doesn't show up in time, the result can be a head-scratchingly bad miss.

Of course, your focus can be even worse, as in those moments when your mind completely checks out and you blow a putt 10 feet past the hole. Severe drops like this often happen when you're tired or hungry. Focus requires energy, plain and simple.

On the flip side, distraction can also come from too much emotion. If any of these sound familiar, the issue is heightened emotion, not wandering attention:

- Focusing on where you don't want the ball to go—
  Chapter 5

- Thinking ahead to calculate what you need for
  a personal best—Chapter 10

- Ruminating about a lip-out or bad break—Chapter 11

- Enjoying how well you're playing more than the details
  of the next shot—Chapter 12

- Thinking about what others are thinking about you—
  Chapter 14

- Doubting the club you selected—Chapter 15
- Replaying past mistakes or bad holes—Chapter 16

If you try to fix a lapse in focus that's caused by emotion, you'll usually intensify the emotion instead. If you're unsure what's driving the issue, remove distractions using the tactics in this chapter. If that doesn't work, you can be confident that emotion—not distraction—is impairing performance. But when a wandering mind isn't caused by low energy or heightened emotion, we need to examine why your focus keeps drifting.

Spotlighting Focus

You know when you're focused and when you're not. But have you ever stopped to think about what focus actually is?

Focus is your primary tool for gathering information that drives good decisions, athletic movement, connection to the shot, improvement, and results. Lapses in focus reduce the amount of information available to you, impairing execution and slowing progress.

The word "distracted" is slightly misleading. You're always focused on something. The problem arises when your focus is pointed in the wrong direction.

Think about the difference between playing in the zone and playing your C-game. In the zone, your mind is full of useful data—slope, wind, lie, moisture—allowing decisions to feel simple and natural. That clarity feeds athleticism and sustains connection to the shot. In your C-game, you're on uninspired autopilot, picking up only what's obvious. You can still hit standard shots, but you struggle with feel, distance control, and adjustment.

Where you direct your focus is determined by your goals and interests. There are countless things competing for your attention beyond the shot at hand: family, work, social media, equipment, fitness, your next golf trip, the club championship, cat videos. Maybe especially the cat videos. Focus is what keeps your mind on a narrow path while blocking out everything else.

Imagine being in a dark room where everything that matters to you is hidden on the walls, floor, and ceiling. You can't see any of it yet, but it's all there. Now imagine turning on a flashlight and sweeping it around. It's time to choose what matters.

You shine the light on golf. Suddenly, everything relevant to your round is illuminated: warming up, alignment, course knowledge, shot selection. Golf becomes your entire world.

That's the power of goals. They point your focus in the right direction and block out what doesn't matter.

What does your focus look like on the course? Does it stay steady for an hour and then fade, like the battery is dying? Is it a wide beam that spreads across too many things at once? A narrow beam that jumps around? Follow where your focus goes and you'll learn what you truly care about while playing.

Ask yourself: What goal is your focus serving? When fun is your main objective, quality golf becomes secondary, and your focus should reflect that. In rounds like this, paying too much attention to shot-making or scoring can actually distract you from enjoying your group.

Still, you're not reading this chapter just to have more fun. You want to hit great shots, play better, lower your handicap, win tournaments, and beat your friends. At the same time, you want to stay connected at work and home, respect your playing partners, and build relationships on the course.

When goals conflict, distraction follows. Not because you lose focus, but because competing priorities pull it in different directions, diverting attention away from what you believe matters most.

Why do you spend time looking for someone else's ball instead of preparing for your shot? Because you value pace of play and being a good partner more than your score. Why don't you ask for quiet when it's your turn to hit? Because you care more about how you're perceived than giving yourself the best chance to execute.

I'm not in the business of deciding what matters to you. I just want you making choices that actually reflect what you want from the game.

Clear Goals Bring Better Focus

You can do more on the course than hit shots. You just need clearer intent. Better focus comes from using your flashlight to illuminate only what serves your goals and leaving everything else in the dark.

If you want to juggle a competitive match, conversation with your partners, emails on your phone, and a swing change, go for it. Just understand how to deploy focus in service of what you want most.

When a round goes south, many golfers make the same mistake. You fail to meet your short-term goal of scoring, lose clarity, and forget that you also want to improve. Poor results distract you from the opportunity to make long-term gains.

You get bad reps, train your mind to accept low-focus shots, strengthen your C-game, and make the same pattern more likely in the future.

Stay connected to the goals that matter to you today, especially when things get difficult. That's how you create momentum you can control. Scoring momentum isn't always available, but process momentum is.

Make sure your goals reflect what you really want and understand why they matter. The "why" adds strength to your focus. Maybe lowering your handicap represents validation for the time and energy you've invested. Maybe winning matters because you love competition or transferring money from your friends' wallets to yours.

Inject your why into moments of distraction, much like Injecting Logic, to refocus quickly. This trains your mind to shift efficiently between conversation, work, and the shot in front of you while still feeding your body the information it needs. It may feel clunky at first, but with repetition it becomes natural.

Here are a few additional ways to reduce distraction:

Have Clear Intent

Choose one goal for the round that supports your long-term objectives. You can't do everything. Your mental whiteboard is only so big. Committing fully to each shot, aiming for the middle of greens, or staying aggressive with birdie putts might serve goals like playing smarter, handling pressure, or lowering your handicap. You might also choose one technical element to integrate. An added benefit is proving you can stay focused on a single objective for an entire round. If you can't, perhaps that becomes your next goal.

Define What's O.B.

Sometimes you can't shut the world out. Before the round, decide what topics or tasks are off-limits and what level of distraction you'll tolerate. Hold yourself accountable and finish knowing you controlled what you could.

Be Honest with Yourself

If you're over the ball trying to convince yourself you aren't distracted, you are. Awareness and denial both take up space on your whiteboard. Distractions have momentum and won't stop unless you act. Step away, clear the board, and refill it only with what matters.

Commit to strengthening focus over many rounds and it will steadily become easier to control. Better focus helps you gather the information needed to choose the right shot. Even then, though, commitment can be difficult.

That's where we're headed next.

KEY TAKEAWAYS

Focus is a tool to gather the information you need to hit quality shots. Make sure it's pointed in the right direction.

Being distracted really means conflicting goals have diverted attention away from what matters most. To improve focus, make clear choices about what you want.

Use the "why" behind your goals to refocus quickly.

CHAPTER 18

Hitting Uncommitted Shots

"I would rather be of clear mind and
decision with the wrong club than with
an unclear mind and the right club."

— WALTER HAGEN

The variety and novelty that golf offers is a big reason you love the game. The sheer volume of variables—wind, firmness, grass length, lies, and undulations, to name a few—means you'll never play the same round twice, even on the same course.

But beneath all that variety, one demand never changes: Every shot requires a decision. Each time you tee it up, the game doesn't just test how well you're hitting it, but how well you make choices and follow through on them. When you're in between clubs, do you hit a full 7-iron or a three-quarter 6? How much will the wind influence the shot? Should you go for it or lay up? Do you aim inside the cup and hit it firm, or play outside the edge with a softer pace? Most shots offer multiple options, challenging your ability to choose one and proceed without hesitation.

Of course, that's easier said than done.

Often, you get stuck between options, unable to make up your mind when hazards and out-of-bounds lurk. The wind is swirling. You're not playing well and don't exactly know where the ball is going. You know the shot you want to hit, you're just unsure whether it'll show up. As you stand over the ball, negative thoughts fuel doubt and emotions, amplifying the challenge. In a match or a tournament, the stakes rise and the fear of making the wrong decision becomes harder to ignore.

Failing to commit is common, even among professionals. What most golfers don't realize is just how costly it is.

When you're uncommitted, your body doesn't have the clear instructions it needs to be athletic. The act of making a decision—whether conscious or intuitive—draws on your experience and prepares your body for a specific motion. When you're stuck between shots, your body doesn't know which movement to organize around. Multiple swing patterns compete for control, as if you're trying to do two different things at once.

A lack of clarity in your mind doesn't guarantee a poor shot, but it makes one far more likely. When you're uncommitted, your misses are bigger, your results are more inconsistent, and your development as a player slows.

The best thing you can do when you can't make up your mind is simple: make a decision. Commitment is binary. You're either committed or you're not. There's no middle ground. To be committed, you don't have to be confident your decision is right. Commitment means removing every other option except one and proceeding as if it's the only choice. That clarity allows you to swing more freely and athletically.

There are times when you try to compensate for being uncommitted by telling yourself to "just commit" or "trust it," but deep down you know you haven't. You decelerate on an approach shot because you fear you have too much club. Instead of swinging decisively toward a sensible target, like the center of the green, you guide the ball toward the flag. On the green, you feel more slope over the ball than you saw behind it and pull the putter face closed. The bottom line is, you can't fake commitment.

Fortunately, the reason many of you struggle to commit is simple: there's something you haven't learned yet.

Think about situations when committing to a shot feels easy, even automatic. On a course you've played many times, you know where to aim off the tee before you even arrive at the first hole, under varying course conditions. You understand how far the ball will run when the fairways are firm and which bunkers you can't carry into the wind. You know the greens so well that some putts don't require a read. You just line up and roll them. You've learned the nuances and are clear about the best options for your game. Commitment comes naturally.

On an unfamiliar course, or in a novel situation at your home club, commitment is harder because you don't yet know what's right. That's why some of you play better with a caddie: You're borrowing their accumulated knowledge and simply doing what you're told.

In theory, every golf shot is unique. In reality, you've hit many similar shots, which makes some decisions easy to commit to. There's little new ground to cover. When you struggle to make a committed decision, you're usually in unfamiliar territory and still learning something about your game, your swing, your emotions, your equipment, or the course itself.

Learning may sound labor-intensive, as if it requires taking notes or making conscious adjustments. That can help and certainly speeds things up, but it isn't required. Learning happens automatically, provided you make a committed decision.

Commitment Unlocks Learning

Each golf shot is like a small research experiment. The cost of indecision is a contaminated sample, like a scientist unknowingly bringing dust into a clean room. When you fail to make a clear decision, you introduce an extra variable that makes the result impossible to interpret. You can't tell whether the shot was off because of incomplete knowledge, a technical flaw, a mental lapse, or because you never fully committed. The feedback is muddled, and the only conclusion you can draw is one you already knew: Hitting an uncommitted shot doesn't work. You've wasted a chance to play better—and to learn.

A committed decision removes that extra variable. Even when the result is poor, the feedback is cleaner and more useful. One wrong decision is an easy price to pay if it helps you avoid several future mistakes. Over time, this clarity dramatically improves both your performance and your understanding of your own game.

Making the wrong decision can still sting, especially in a big moment. To avoid being wrong, you may hesitate or hedge. But indecision guarantees only one thing: you can't be right.

Your best odds of success come from being committed, a perspective that instantly removes the pressure to get it right. Of course you want to choose wisely, but you'll do that more often when your feedback isn't contaminated by indecision.

Treat moments of indecision as a signal that there's something to learn, then make the best decision you can. Take advantage of the opportunity. You might be right and hit a great shot. Or you might be wrong and gain useful information you can fold into your game in a natural, effortless way. As discussed in Chapter 3, golf without learning becomes stagnant and less enjoyable. By making committed decisions, you create a steady stream of learning that keeps your motivation, interest, and passion for the game alive.

Every time you make a clear decision, you also strengthen your ability to be decisive. One reason indecision lingers is that many golfers unknowingly train themselves to swing with multiple options in mind. Consider a simple example: a par-3 with a quartering wind, where you're between clubs. If you fully commit to a smooth 6-iron and see how it reacts to that wind, you learn something concrete about your ball flight. If you hedge and swing tentatively, the result teaches you nothing.

It's okay to be unsure which decision is best. The goal isn't to eliminate uncertainty; it's to commit despite it. Train an intolerance for indecision without slowing your pace of play. That may mean trusting your instincts more. But the more forcefully you decide, the more committed you'll be over the ball.

Finally, watch for a subtler source of indecision that appears when you push the upper edge of your ability. Learning mistakes—the kind that only show up when you're stretching your skills—often create uncertainty. A recent swing change may behave differently from uneven lies. Fatigue may require more club than your stock yardages suggest. These lessons can elevate your game, but they also introduce new considerations. Don't let them derail your commitment.

As you become more willing to commit and learn from the outcome, another obstacle remains: how you evaluate your decisions after the round. Many golfers fall victim to a powerful bias that quietly reinforces indecision. That's what we'll tackle next.

KEY TAKEAWAYS

Making a clear decision provides your body with the instructions it needs to be athletic. Being stuck between shots is like trying to do two things at once.

Commitment is binary—you're either committed or you're not. You might be unsure your choice is right. That's okay. The challenge is committing despite not knowing.

Committing guarantees improvement and learning.

CHAPTER 19

Coulda, Woulda, Shoulda

"One reason golf is such an exasperating game is
that a thing we learned is so easily forgotten, and we find
ourselves struggling year after year with faults we
had discovered and corrected time and again."

— BOBBY JONES

Listen to the stories golfers share after their round and you'll hear a common refrain that goes something like this: "I played okay, shot 87, but it could have easily been an 83." They went brain-dead on the fifth with a stupid three-putt from eight feet. Hit driver instead of 3-wood on nine—straight into the hazard. Failed to get up and down on three easy chips. Hit one out of bounds on 16 and lipped out a five-footer on 17. The details vary but the theme is the same: "If only I had (fill in the blank), my score would have been so much better."

You'll even hear players who just shot their lowest round ever count the strokes they could have avoided, the wasted shots they would have saved by playing smarter, or the putts they should have hit harder. Coulda, woulda, shoulda. The fact is, you didn't.

While examining your rounds like this may seem driven by a desire to improve—or simply like friendly banter—it's actually blocking you from lowering your scores. Of course there's value in reviewing mistakes and finding areas to work on. But that's not what's happening here. You're erasing shots from your mind, as if they can be easily avoided on the course. They can't. Losing strokes the same way again and again proves it. This is revisionist history, plain and simple.

Spoiler alert: You're not as good as your post-round commentary would lead you to believe. You're not yet skilled enough to avoid all those poor shots, bad decisions, three-putts, and penalty strokes. You may be eventually, but those extra shots are firmly within your current bell curve. They reflect the quality of golfer you are right now.

They also stick around longer since you're not proactively figuring out how to improve. Next round, you'll say something similar—lamenting wasted shots, missed opportunities, looking back at what now seems obvious, wishing your score was lower. The pattern repeats.

The nature of this reflection is best characterized by a problem called Hindsight Bias.[9] After the round, you have the results. Only with that knowledge does hindsight show where you could have saved shots. If you knew that ahead of time ... well, that would make you a psychic.

Hindsight is 20/20 because of this informational advantage. You now know you needed to take an extra club, play more break, reset after getting distracted, or slow down your takeaway. You may have suspected what choice was better or how you could have executed better, but you didn't act on it. The trick is developing that crystal-clear vision before you hit the shot, not after.

Perfection in golf is a moving target. There's always more to improve. Your mistakes reflect that. You would have produced a better outcome in the first place if you could have. And yes, the Hindsight Bias prevents your hard-won experience from being put to good use.

The Hindsight Bias doesn't occur randomly. You may have picked up the habit from listening to other players vent, not realizing the impact on your game. Or you're making the fatal assumption that knowing what you did wrong means knowing how to correct it. Recognition is an important first step, but don't confuse it for a correction.

If this bias has stuck around long enough to be noticeable, it's serving a purpose. In the short run, it offers comfort. But it's counterproductive. You might be shaving a few shots off the top to lessen the pain of a bad round, avoid thinking about how much you need to improve, or make your game look better to other players.

Commonly, it also protects your confidence: You want to believe you're a better player than you are right now, or that your C-game isn't as weak as it is. You don't want to think of yourself as capable of bleeding shots so easily or making simple mistakes. If this applies to you, revisit Chapter 12 or 13 to stabilize your confidence.

Hindsight only helps if it leads to foresight. Otherwise it's just a wish. You need to think proactively about how to be better in the future. Or, you might have to admit you're more interested in feeling good than actually playing better.

Turning Hindsight into Foresight

Regardless of why you've fallen into the Hindsight Bias trap, you can immediately get yourself out by adding one word as you question your play post-round: how.

How could you have made a different decision? How could you have hit a better chip? How could you have convinced yourself to go back to the cart and change clubs? Framing easily lost shots like this forces your mind to think practically and unlocks knowledge the Hindsight Bias was blocking.

This change can help you avoid some common mistakes right away. However, if you notice many areas that need work, be selective. Some improvements, like overhauling your swing mechanics or fixing a long-standing tempo issue, require sustained effort and can't be tackled all at once. Real progress doesn't happen overnight, and there's only so much you can do simultaneously.

Try this instead: After each of your next several rounds, note the reasons you're losing shots. Focus on mistakes that can save you strokes with little effort, or on the single most costly error. For example, if you're consistently leaving 30-foot putts five feet short, practice distance control until you're reliably two-putting. If you're pulling driver when you know 3-wood is smarter, learn to recognize when overconfidence overrides prudent shot selection. Then make that your primary point of focus until you're saving those shots with ease. Too often players remember the lesson on the 17th hole, not on the first tee where it could make a real difference.

After each round, review only what you're trying to improve, noting progress and examining how to be better. You can identify other reasons you lost shots, but put them aside for the future. This way you get the needed repetitions and reduce the chance for mistakes or bad habits to reoccur.

Worst case, if you attempt to improve deliberately and don't make progress, you'll at least have evidence you've reached the limits of your current ability and can look for an instructor to help. In the end, the choice is simple: Spend your time talking about how you coulda, woulda, shoulda saved strokes, or figure out how to actually do it.

When you bleed strokes on the same hole—one you now describe as your nemesis—the benefit of hindsight may not provide all the answers. These holes can leave a lasting impression. The tactics I describe next can help you escape the past.

KEY TAKEAWAYS

Hindsight is 20/20 because after the round, you have the results. If you knew them ahead of time, you'd be a psychic.

Ask yourself "how" questions to think more practically about how to avoid mistakes and play better.

CHAPTER 20

Holes That Have Your Number

"Success depends almost entirely
on how effectively you learn to manage
the game's two ultimate adversaries:
the course and yourself."

— JACK NICKLAUS

Like all good competitors, the course can challenge your limits, test your composure, and push you to raise your game. It often wins, occasionally so dramatically it leaves a mark.

Certain holes seem to own you. Tension rises just thinking about them. Often, it's the most demanding ones that get in your head. There's no place to bail out—O.B. right, trees left, blind approach, forced carry, water in front, tricky green. Enough penal features to make you wonder if the hole was designed specifically to torture you.

Some have trees that seem to pull your ball like magnets. On others, the trouble sits exactly where you tend to miss. Tee shots that don't fit your eye, but seduce you to do more, like forcing a ball flight to match the shape of the hole. Even easy holes can psych you out. The short par-4 you should birdie, the wide fairway you somehow can't find. Each misstep adds another layer of frustration and dread.

Whether it's a specific hole, a type of shot, or even a playing condition—wet fairways, crosswinds from the left—you're fighting the past as much as the present.

Memories of previous disasters flash through your mind. Nerves amp up. Negative thoughts spring to mind. Focus is drawn toward trouble. You try to make a good swing, hoping for the best. But hope isn't a strategy. You can't help but be quick and jerky, even when you've been playing well up to that point in the round.

These nightmarish holes and menacing shots don't have to be your undoing. Nor do they have to carry over from round to round or lead to lasting scars. Ideally, built-up tension dissipates within minutes of leaving the course, or within a few hours after a particularly rough day. Either way, the next time you tee it up, you're reset.

But emotions are messy. Sometimes they get stuck, leaving behind what I call "accumulated emotion." Despite your best "fresh start" intentions, carried-over emotions lurk beneath the surface, undermining your ability to be present, focused, and confident. With this excess emotion there from the start, any new emotion can quickly push you over the edge, decreasing the odds you'll catch the rise in emotion early enough to retain control.

Any of the emotions I've discussed in previous chapters can accumulate. You can minimize this by applying the strategy I laid out in Chapter 6: changing your perspective, Injecting Logic, and chipping away at your emotional reaction in real time.

After particularly intense rounds that won't let go, take time to write about the lingering emotion, or talk it through with a coach, trusted playing partner, or friend. Then apply the correct perspective or logic again. Sometimes when your mind remains flooded with emotion after the round is over, the right perspective is hard to accept. You have to release the emotion before you regain the ability to think logically.

This applies after good rounds too. The accumulation of positive emotion—excitement, relief, vindication—is a prime reason players can't string together consecutive great scores.

While this tactic works for recent emotion, what about the holes, shots, putts, even rounds that have made a lasting impression? It's tough to play well when these wounds won't heal. The raw emotion stays close to the surface, ready to erupt at the slightest trigger. You're easily overwhelmed by reactions that seem irrational, paralyzing your ability to focus on today's shot and inviting your old swing to return. You may break free temporarily, but each time you succumb, the pattern strengthens.

The adage that time heals all wounds? Not in golf. Ask any golfer still haunted by a playoff choke from five years ago. What matters is what you do with that time. The good news is, there is a practical way forward.

Working Through Scar Tissue

The body has a way to protect us from further injury, but that protection comes at a cost. After an injury, the body quickly produces a patch to help protect the surrounding area in the short term. Without treatment or rehab over the long term, however, that patch hardens into scar tissue[10]—rigid, inflexible, limiting your range of motion.

In the same way, the brain helps you cope with painful experience through denial, excuse-making, and other proactive measures. These strategies can be useful in the short term, but when relied upon too long they interfere with the brain's ability to fully process the memory. The result is an unprocessed memory that continues to carry its original charge. Memories ideally are matter of fact.

You might remember topping your tee shot on the first hole of a playoff—the shock, the embarrassment—but you shouldn't still feel it today. Just as you have to rebuild healthy muscle in the body by working through the scar tissue directly, you must do the same with these emotional scars.

Past experience should be an asset that you leverage to play better. Instead, these scars become liabilities that grind your game down. To convert old failures into assets that drive your game higher, you need to extract the lessons from them.

Unlike other tactics presented in this book, progress doesn't start on the golf course. You need a quiet place where you can relax. In many instances, the wound isn't deep. Once you examine it directly, the pressure releases easily. Sometimes the emotion runs deeper. Working through it is like a deep tissue massage. It's uncomfortable, even painful, but effective. Ideally, transformative.

Here's how to begin:

Take a sheet of paper and write a headline that captures the situation. For example, "I chunk it in the water on 15 every time I'm in good position off the tee." Then start writing about the situation in detail, including the emotional pain. These experiences are vivid; describe what stands out. The splash as the ball hits water. The heavy thud of the club digging behind the ball. The frustration as you fish another ball from your bag.

You might find the specific instance that started it all, or discover it's the cumulative weight of repetition. Either way, chronicle what happened, how you felt, where the emotions intensified, and any associated thoughts.

Once the story is clear, ask yourself, "Why is this so painful? Why has it stuck with me?" Emotion often hangs around because you have something to learn, and this is your chance to understand more.

Your answers will reveal a faulty perspective. Perhaps you're more focused on the outcome. You often have a good round going into this hole, and that's made you anxious and less diligent in your decision-making. Or, you have unreasonable expectations of your iron play, and on other holes the cost isn't as high. You can't see the forest when you're lost in the trees. If the insight doesn't come immediately, step away. Come back in a few days. Sometimes lessons need time to surface.

Once you've found a clearer perspective, you're ready for the next step: replacing the negative muscle memory. Use a positive memory to replace the old muscle memory.

In a relaxed setting, envision the haunting hole, but this time, imagine hitting an optimal shot. Find a memory where you've hit that exact shot successfully, at a different time, maybe on a different hole, but the same shot.

Strengthen this memory. Imagine it vividly and bring it back to life by focusing on the physical details of setting up, taking the club back, the sound and feel of contact, the ball's flight path. Use whatever sensory details come most naturally. Do this several times, breathing deeply to strengthen the connection.

Then massage this ideal shot into the haunting situation, replacing the old memory with the new one.

Visualization alone rarely cures these demons. It begins the process, instills something positive, builds momentum. The biggest opportunity comes on the course the next time you're on that hole. While getting ready to hit, take an extra moment with that ideal shot. Let it hold your attention—toward your target, toward success—rather than dwell on past failures or what to avoid.

You might see immediate improvement. Or at least a shot that sucks less. That's progress. If not, limit the self-criticism. More reps are needed. This process is like chopping down a tree. Each swing matters, even when progress isn't immediately visible. Eventually, the tree falls.

When you make progress here and elsewhere in your mental game, you'll find "the zone" more often. But finding it isn't enough. You want to stay there. The next chapter will show you how.

KEY TAKEAWAYS

Emotions are messy and can leave behind "accumulated emotion." They undermine your ability to be present, and any new emotion can quickly push you over the edge.

After intense rounds, you have to release emotion before you regain the ability to think logically. Try writing or talking.

Unprocessed memories trap emotion. "Massage" through mental scar tissue by instilling memories of positive swings to steadily change how you handle haunting situations.

CHAPTER 21

Falling Out of the Zone

*"Golf is a funny game; sometimes the
ball just finds the hole when your
mind is calm and your body is ready."*

— CHI CHI RODRIGUEZ

The advice in this book can help you enter that elusive, mystical place called "the zone."

Arriving there grants exceptional abilities. A calm mind. A swing that feels natural, athletic, and effortless. Automatic commitment to your target with no doubts or concerns about swing or score. Dialed in, executing shots as you envision them with quiet confidence.

When you're in the zone, bad breaks don't affect you. Missed opportunities don't faze you. You're fully in the present. Deeply immersed in the experience of playing the game, being with friends, and enjoying the world around you.

This heightened state can't happen all the time. You can't find "it" with your mental game any more than you can find "it" with your swing. However, as your B- and C-game advance, and the gap between them and your A-game narrows, the path for you to play some amazing golf gets shorter and easier.

Unfortunately, the zone is fragile. Like walking a tightrope, the slightest wobble causes you to fall. You seem to arrive without knowing how and slip out without knowing why. Reaching it is delightful; staying there is a dream.

Despite its mysterious nature, the zone doesn't occur randomly. It's predictable, as are the reasons you fall out. The challenge is controlling the elements that can differ from day to day. That kind of command is a primary focus of elite players. They've turned a tightrope into a balance beam.

To make it easier to stay in the zone and quickly find your way back, let's look at a few reasons, beyond what I've discussed in Part II, that can lead to losing it.

Losing Energy

The zone cannot be reached or sustained without the right amount of energy. It's as simple as that. If your level of energy is too high or too low, you might be able to perform well, but you won't reach the zone. As I discussed in Chapter 6, the Yerkes-Dodson Law provides us with a visual to reinforce this relationship.

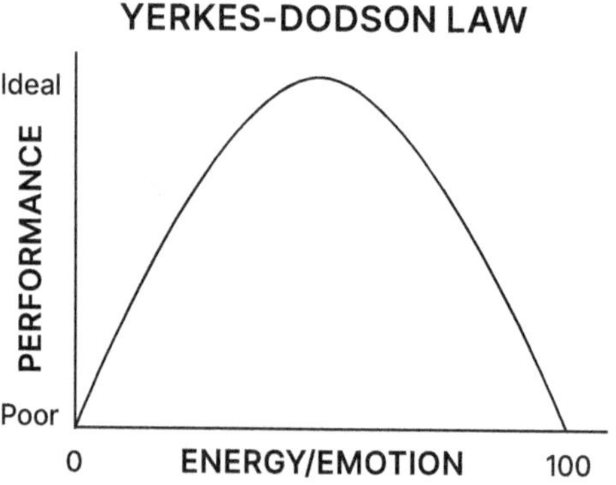

Once you find the right amount of energy, sustaining it is a challenge. Despite that calm composure, the zone uses a lot of energy, making fatigue a prime reason for slipping out. Physical energy is part of that, and in general, playing golf burns more than many golfers realize—even riding in a cart can burn 300 calories per hour[11]—so be sure that you're hydrated and fed.

Mental energy is a factor too. Decisions require energy, and a wide gap between your A-game and C-game consumes even more. You use more energy on knowledge and skills that have yet to reach Unconscious Competence than on what's already there. Mastery is energy-efficient. The narrower the gap in your bell curve, the more you've mastered, and less energy is needed to access recently acquired knowledge and skills.

If you notice that you feel a bit tired, but know that you're hydrated and fed, you can generate mental energy by tapping into the "why" behind your goals. As laid out in Chapter 17, your why can help to improve focus. In the same way, it can also help you dig deep to find a boost of energy, like a runner getting a second wind. Not only can it help you get back in the zone, it can also help you build mental strength and endurance, making it easier to stay there before fatigue kicks you out.

When you slip out of the zone, first check your energy level. This is the most important element. Without it, the other two that I'll discuss aren't relevant.

The Game Feels Too Easy

Even if you have the right energy, you also need to be sufficiently challenged to find the zone. This element was detailed by Mihaly Csikszentmihalyi, a Hungarian psychology professor, in his popular book *Flow: The Psychology of Optimal Experience*.

He defines being in the zone as a state of "flow" and asserts that to reach this state, the performer needs to be both challenged and skilled enough to meet that challenge.

You can access the zone at any skill level if you're equally challenged. This is why it can be tough to play your best against weak competition on an easy course, or against tough opposition at Oakmont.

Perspective matters, and a shift can easily alter your sense of how well your competence matches the demand. Case in point: Playing in the zone can make the game feel too easy, exposing an expectation that excellent golf will continue. The lack of perceived challenge causes just enough of a drop in focus to kick you out. The mind is built for efficiency and doesn't waste effort. When the game feels too easy, you ignore the little details offered up by the zone, like subtleties in the green that can make the line appear before you as if drawn with a laser.

The mind is a powerful tool, and a shift in perspective can get you back. Kill the expectation. Embrace the challenge of sustaining the zone. While the game may feel easy, take a moment to recognize there's no ease behind the scenes—like a duck gliding serenely across the water while paddling furiously underneath.

Extra Aware of How Well You're Playing

Playing at a level beyond what you're typically capable of is noteworthy and gets your attention—just enough to be distracting.

You're suddenly attuned to how well you're performing and what's different in your process, pacing, or swing. You think about your commitment to the decision versus just committing to it. You're aware of your pace walking to the ball, not just walking. You focus more on positions in your swing that feel noticeably good, not just swinging. Score stands out too, and you might envision a career low or ask about the course record.

Beyond focusing too much on score or swing, as I discussed in Chapters 9 and 10, this extra awareness is an attempt to learn. You're trying to figure out what you're doing well so you can find your way back again. Except, as I discussed in Chapter 16, the zone, or even your A-game, includes aspects that are too new for you to control.

Rather than analyzing what's working mid-round, reflect after the round to see what might be usable in the future. In the meantime, let yourself play and leave the learning for later. You can't actively learn and play your best simultaneously. Those are two very different mentalities. The good news is that even if these extra thoughts have taken you out of the zone, you're still not far away.

If your extra awareness also includes being surprised by how well you're playing, part of you doesn't think highly enough of your game. You're not surprised by things you expect. You don't blink when your neighbor knocks on the door. Tiger Woods? That would surprise you.

To play this well, you must be capable of it. Clearly your perception of yourself is off, and it's okay to be a bit forceful in reminding yourself of that. Believe it. You can play this well. It's not random. You weren't body-snatched by someone else. This is the peak of your ability—own it. The less notable it becomes, the more comfortable you'll be staying in the zone.

Whether or not you've started to get into the zone more often, the mental game is an ever-evolving and challenging puzzle. If you've struggled to find a breakthrough, the next chapter can help.

KEY TAKEAWAYS

The zone doesn't occur randomly. It's predictable, as are the reasons you fall out. The challenge is controlling the elements that can differ from day to day.

When you're tired, you can generate mental energy by tapping into the "why" behind your goals.

When golf feels easy, keep your perspective sharp by recognizing there's no ease behind the scenes.

When self-awareness rises, remember you can't actively learn and play your best simultaneously. Play golf and learn later.

CHAPTER 22

Sharpening Your Perspective

"There is nothing in this game of golf that
can't be improved upon if you practice."
— PATTY BERG

Like the golf swing, the mental game has too many moving pieces to be covered comprehensively in a single book. My goal here has been more modest and, I hope, more useful: Address the most common mental challenges golfers face with enough depth to help you make real progress.

As you apply what you've learned, however, you may find yourself stuck, frustrated, or unsure whether you're actually moving forward. Before assuming this new approach isn't helping, it's worth troubleshooting a few common reasons progress can feel elusive.

Be Sure Your Assessment Is Right

You may be improving without realizing it. Increased awareness is progress. It's a necessary first step that eventually leads to tangible change. Seeing more clearly what's happening in your mind, even when it's uncomfortable, is not a step backward.

If, after a month of focused effort, nothing seems to be changing, one of two things is usually true. Either you're missing an important piece and need to reassess, or the changes in your mentality haven't been reinforced strongly enough to show up during a round. Much like a swing change that works on the range but falls apart on the course, a new mental approach often needs more time and repetition before it holds up under pressure.

Too Many Problems to Correct

By now, you may have identified several areas you want to improve. Since you can't take on everything at once—your whiteboard is only so big—you need to prioritize. Here are three practical ways to decide where to start:

Start Small

Smaller problems are often easier to fix. Early wins build confidence and momentum, which makes it easier to tackle larger issues later.

Go Big

You might instead choose the problem that causes the most damage, the one costing you the most shots, triggering the strongest emotions, or dragging your C-game far below where it should be. Progress here is slower, but the payoff is substantial. Strengthening your floor raises your ceiling.

Confidence First

If anger, fear, and overconfidence all plague your game, start with confidence. It's the foundation of the mental game. Weak confidence amplifies other issues; stable confidence tends to soften them. The reverse isn't always true. Learning to manage fear, for example, doesn't automatically build confidence.

If you're still unsure, just get started. Try something to learn something. You can't figure everything out standing outside the ropes.

Overloaded with Data

As your awareness of the mental game grows, you may notice that you're noticing too much. Patterns in yourself, your playing partners, even strangers on the course jump out at you. Your mind becomes a sponge, absorbing information faster than it can process it.

When that sponge is saturated, concentration suffers. You may feel mentally exhausted, miss obvious cues, or struggle to stay present. While the constant focus can feel productive, you're likely waiting for it to translate into lower scores.

Fortunately, the solution is straightforward. Just as your body digests food, your brain needs to digest information. Writing things down during practice, mid-round, or afterwards helps clear mental clutter faster. Talking through what you're noticing works too. You don't even need to review your notes. The act of getting thoughts out of your head creates clarity on its own.

When Intense Emotions Seem to Come Out of Nowhere

When strong emotions catch you off guard, it's usually for one of three reasons.

First, you may not yet recognize the early warning signs. These can include specific thoughts, physical sensations, lapses in focus, breakdowns in shot selection, or recurring swing patterns. Careful attention during the round—and honest review afterwards—builds awareness of these signals.

Second, you may be highly skilled at suppressing or numbing emotion. If so, you don't notice feelings until they erupt. Watch for the behaviors you use to keep emotions at bay: complaining to a partner, walking faster, withdrawing, or hunting for distraction. These are often signs that emotion is already rising.

Finally, emotions such as fear, anger, impatience, or doubt may have accumulated over years. When a situation arises today, old emotion floods in and overwhelms you instantly. It's not a fair fight. Review Chapter 20 for a method to reduce the weight of these stored emotions.

Your C-Game Is Worse Than You Thought

Ideally, you'd apply these tools and improve right away. Sometimes the opposite happens. Focus functions like a magnifier; it reveals flaws more clearly, which can temporarily make performance worse. This is common at the stage of Conscious Incompetence. You're more aware, but not yet skilled.

As you look more closely, you may discover your problems are deeper or more complex than you believed. What you thought was your C-game may turn out to be closer to an F-game. That realization can sting. But it also explains why your A-game doesn't show up very often and hasn't reached the heights you expected. The upside is clarity. You now understand what's been holding you back, and that understanding gives you a real chance to become the golfer you imagined.

The Intersection of Golf and Life

You might be confident, decisive, and emotionally balanced in the rest of your life. So why doesn't that carry over to golf?

One reason is compression. A single round of golf can contain more emotional swings than a month of normal life. There's little time to process, reflect, or recover. Without that space, emotions are amplified, and familiar coping strategies fall short. Golf demands a distinct skill set.

It's also possible that unresolved personal issues surface on the course, even if they remain hidden elsewhere. Golf has a way of exposing fear, insecurity, and old frustration, especially when you've invested so much time, money, identity, and expectation into the game. If personal issues are holding your performance hostage, working with a therapist can be a productive step.

The Shanks and the Yips

The shanks and the yips are complex and, unfortunately, beyond the scope of this book. That said, the process outlined in Chapter 20 can be a useful starting point. It addresses the emotional scars that interfere with integrating sound technique. Chapters 8 and 9 can then help reduce overthinking and make it easier to carry improvements from practice to the course.

At some point, understanding stops being the hard part. The progress comes from repetition, patience, and trust. That's rarely glamorous. But it's how lasting change actually happens.

Sharpening Your Ax

There's no magic cure for mental-game problems. If there were, it would cost more than this book. The magic comes from repetition and taking advantage of each opportunity to step onto the course.

The key is readiness. A refrain emphasized by the famous non-golfer Abraham Lincoln, who said, "Give me six hours to chop down a tree and I will spend the first four sharpening the ax." This metaphorical pearl relates nicely to the mental game of golf.

What I've aimed to offer you is a sharper perspective and the willingness to swing it consistently. Each swing builds strength. Each cut goes deeper, clearing years of mental overgrowth that's been choking your potential.

Building a new mentality doesn't require special talent. Only consistent effort. You're ready. Not perfect, but ready to make progress, play better, and enjoy the game more.

Once you start, keep chopping until each problem comes down. Don't stop halfway. When an old issue finally falls, it becomes the lumber you use to build something stronger: better decisions, improved feel, smarter shot-making, greater competitiveness, or simply a clearer, calmer presence on the course.

Inch by inch, potential becomes reality.

You can accelerate the process through cross-training. The traders, poker players, entrepreneurs, executives, and other high performers I work with wrestle with the same mental challenges. Apply these concepts beyond golf and you'll get more reps—and faster results.

This process doesn't end with the last page. It continues every time you step onto the course with intention, patience, and a sharpened ax.

Endnotes

CHAPTER 4: Changing Your Mindset is Easy

1 The origin is uncertain. Attribution is often given to Abraham Maslow, as well as Dr. Thomas Gordon. It's also known as the Four Stages of Learning or the Conscious Competency Model. Cited in: McHugh, Donald E. 2004. Golf and the game of leadership: an 18-hole guide for success in business and life. New York, NY: AMACOM.

CHAPTER 6: Technique to Control Emotions

2 Amy Arnsten, Carolyn M. Mazure & Rajita Sinha, "Everyday Stress Can Shut Down the Brain's Chief Command Center," *Scientific American*, April 2012, Vol. 306, No.4, pp. 48–53.

3 Robert M. Yerkes & John D. Dodson, "The relation of strength of stimulus to rapidity of habit-formation," *Journal of Comparative Neurology and Psychology*, November 1908, Vol. 18, Issue 5, pp. 459–482.

CHAPTER 9: Overthinking Technique

4 George A. Miller's 1956 paper, "The Magical Number Seven, Plus or Minus Two: Some Limits on Our Capacity for Processing Information"

CHAPTER 11: Overreacting to Bad Breaks

5 Abigail Tucker, "Are Babies Born Good?," *Smithsonian Magazine*, January 2013, https://www.smithsonianmag.com/science-nature/are-babies-born-good-165443013/?c=y&story=fullstory.

CHAPTER 12: Overconfidence

6   Zell, Ethan & Strickhouser, Jason & Sedikides, Constantine & Alicke, Mark. (2019). The Better-Than-Average Effect in Comparative Self-Evaluation: A Comprehensive Review and Meta-Analysis. Psychological Bulletin. 146. 118-149. 10.1037 /bul0000218.

CHAPTER 16: The Frustration of Playing Poorly

7   Daniel Kahneman & Amos Tversky, "Prospect Theory: An Analysis of Decision under Risk," *Econometrica*, Econometric Society, March 1979, Vol. 47, No. 2, pp. 263–292.

8   Amos Tversky & Daniel Kahneman, "Advances in Prospect Theory: Cumulative Representation of Uncertainty," *Journal of Risk and Uncertainty*, Kluwer Academic Publishers, 1992.

CHAPTER 19: Coulda, Woulda, Shoulda

9   Roese, N. J., & Vohs, K. D. (2012). Hindsight Bias. *Perspectives on Psychological Science*, 7(5), 411-426.

CHAPTER 20: Holes That Have Your Number

10   Gurtner, G. C., Werner, S., Barrandon, Y., & Longaker, M. T. (2008). *Wound repair and regeneration*. Nature, 453(7193), 314–321.

CHAPTER 21: Falling Out of the Zone

11   Pennington, Bill. 2010. "A Little Scientific Research for All Those 19th-Hole Debates." *On Par* (blog), August 1, 2010. The New York Times.

Acknowledgments

Writing is challenging for me. I'm dyslexic, so I rely heavily on others for help. I'm immensely grateful to everyone who contributed to this book.

First and foremost, my writing partner Beth Kupchinsky. Thank you for your unwavering dedication to this project. I couldn't have completed this book without you. It's so hard for me to dig ideas out of my head on my own. Your questions, insights, and perspectives helped bring this material to light.

I also want to thank Dr. Bob Rotella, and others who established the field of golf psychology, for their pioneering work. It's an honor to follow in the footsteps of giants.

To all the clients I've worked with over the years, thank you for helping me to become a better coach. In your own way, each of you forced me to raise my game so I could help you raise yours.

Thank you to the listeners of *The Sweet Spot Podcast*, members of Shadow Wood Country Club, and friends and family who completed a lengthy survey that helped me learn about the psychological nuances of different types of golfers. Your thoughtful responses were greatly appreciated.

Thank you to the members and staff at Jericho National Golf Club whose humor, conversations, and countless rounds together—both knowingly and unknowingly—helped bring this material to life.

Golf has been part of my family since I was a kid, first learning the game from my grandparents, David and Marie, using clubs far too big and heavy. They're not around to see this book come to fruition but knew how grateful I was for teaching me this amazing game.

My parents, Bob and Debby, have always been my biggest supporters. Constantly cheering me on, spending hours watching me play, and lending an ear when I needed one. I'm so grateful for their love, encouragement, and belief in me every step of the way.

To my family and friends, thank you for your support and for understanding that working on this book often came at the expense of time we would otherwise have spent together—including on the golf course. Especially my wife Corey, who pushed me to write this book. I'm so happy you did. This was an incredible experience. I'm so grateful to have you, and our beautiful daughter Teddy, in my corner.

About the Author

Jared Tendler, MS, LMHC, is an internationally recognized mental game coach with over 20 years of experience. His clients span 45 countries and include everyday golfers, as well as PGA Tour and LPGA Tour winners, world champion poker players, executives, entrepreneurs, lawyers, and financial traders. In addition to *Everyday Golf Psychology*, Jared is also the author of three best-selling books, *The Mental Game of Trading*, and *The Mental Game of Poker 1 & 2*.

As a junior golfer, Jared dreamed of playing professionally, and his interest in golf psychology began after choking in the U.S. Open local qualifier in 1997—missing four short putts and a playoff by one shot. While playing collegiate golf for Division III Skidmore College, Jared was a three-time All-American and won nine tournaments but continually underperformed in national events. Driven to find better answers, he earned a master's degree in counseling psychology and became a licensed therapist. In 2005, Jared started working with golfers to develop a practical, straightforward approach to golf psychology, helping players at every level, from tournament professionals to beginners.

Proving his clients aren't the only ones to benefit from his system, Jared solved his own issues and in 2013 qualified for the U.S. Mid-Amateur, shooting two-under. Currently, he's a member at Jericho National Golf Club in New Hope, PA, regularly plays in regional tournaments, and now dreams of playing in the U.S. Senior Open.

Want More?

I provide regular advice through
my blog, social media, newsletter,
and interviews.

To connect, learn more, and
stay up on the latest, go to:
www.jaredtendler.com.